ADVANCE PRAISE

"*Ball Gowns to Yoga Pants* is a must read for any aspiring or established business owner. Running a business is not for the faint of heart. You must be willing to do the work. Author Dr. Shellie Hipsky not only shows you how to turn your passion into a business, but she also gives the steps needed to make sure your enterprise is successful!"

—**Allison Maslan**, CEO of Pinnacle Global Network and Wall Street Journal Bestselling Author of *Scale or Fail: How to Build Your Dream Team, Explode Your Growth and Let Your Business Soar*

"Open the cover of this book only if you are prepared to open your mind and your heart to the work of manifesting your greatest potential to live your best life! In this highly entertaining and deeply engaging book, Dr. Shellie takes the reader on a guided journey from their WHY to their HOW by sharing her own story, woven among insights shared by a multitude of successful entrepreneurs and leaders. If you are ready to be inspired, and to do the work you were born to do, turn the first page of this book and begin."

—**Judy Safern**, President of Leading Thinkers

"Gain insight on how to speak your truth and stand in your power. Current and future entrepreneurs will learn tips and techniques to help them stay grounded, focused, and centered through the peaks and valleys of building a business while maintaining your sanity and confidence."

—**Lucinda Cross**, President of Activate World Wide, Inc.

"Entrepreneurship is a journey, and it is never a straight path, but instead, it is filled with many forks in the road. However, Dr. Shellie is sharing her years of experiences to help others have a smoother journey. I would highly recommend entrepreneurs and small business owners take full advantage and, most importantly, LISTEN & LEARN as Dr. Shellie has provided you the guidebook—*Ball Gowns to Yoga Pants*. Get your pen ready as you will want to take copious notes!"

—**Debbie Saviano**, Founder of
Women's Leadership LIVE

"Ball Gowns to Yoga Pants: Entrepreneurial Secrets to Creating Your Dream Business and Brand is more than a business book of training tips. Dr. Shellie Hipsky brings her readers into her inner-circle and includes them in her journey. She shares her vulnerabilities and allows them to know her. She asks thought-provoking questions that make her readers pause and get to know themselves. Most importantly, Dr. Shellie redefines the term 'female entrepreneur' so women everywhere feel that they too can create a business from the ground up, no matter who they are, how many hats they wear or how little business experience they've had. In short, Shellie helps her readers realize that they matter and that they have value and skills to offer the world—that realization is priceless."

—**Haseena Patel**, Author; International speaker;
Cofounder and Executive Director of LNGB
International, based in South Africa

"As a new entrepreneur, Dr. Shellie's *Balls Gowns to Yoga Pants* is the book that I will carry with me throughout the year. The stories, applications, and gems dropped serve as an inspiring blueprint. Whether you're starting a new business, refining your current business, or have a desire to better navigate your personal and professional journeys, this book is your ultimate guide."

—**Dr. Atiya Abdelmalik**, Community Engagement Practitioner of HCD Consulting, LLC

"If you are starting a business or thinking about starting one, you MUST read this book! In *Ball Gowns to Yoga Pants*, Dr. Shellie shares her entrepreneurial journey and the lessons she learned along the way. Throughout the book, she stops and poses questions designed to make you think about your business. She talks about very practical, fundamental issues that every business owner should consider in the early stages. The problem is that we don't know that we should be thinking about these things! Thanks, Dr. Shellie, for creating a book that will help business owners avoid the mistakes we made early in our journey!"

—**Meg Huwar**, Principal, Brand Accelerator Podcaster, Marketing Monday's with Meg

"I was blown away by all the powerful strategies that Dr. Shellie revealed! With all the insider tips and action steps that connect you to your mission and vision, it will propel your business to new heights and to all the outcomes you desire! This step-by-step roadmap will lead you to and through the transformation that you've been waiting for!"

—**Donna Palamar**, International Empowerment & Lifestyle Coach, WOmentum BuildHERs

"Dr. Shellie engages the reader with questions that prompt us to consider those inquiries with thoughtful authenticity. Insight from experts, punctuated by her own accounts, and then followed by interactive and conversational prompts. This flow and method allow for a beautiful introspection that I find both pleasurable and valuable."

—**Kym Gable**, TV News Anchor/Reporter of KDKA-TV and Vision and Voice

"In her much anticipated 13th book, *Ball Gowns to Yoga Pants*, Dr. Shellie slashes through the intimidation of entrepreneurship with her razor-sharp stilettos and one-of-a-kind storytelling, making you feel like you are sitting with her in your living room, sharing a cup of coffee and conversation while conquering the world. *BGYP* is enticing and honest and leaves the audience feeling capable. Build your life on your terms by starting on page 1 with Dr. Shellie, and don't look back."

—**Anna Compton**, Film/Entertainment Publicist of Ovation PR and Advertising

"This book not only inspires you to think bigger and go after your dreams. It also helps you believe that it's truly possible for you to reach your goals no matter how big they are. Dr. Shellie Hipsky shares a very practical step-by-step framework to allow you to start taking massive inspired action toward your goals! This book is a must for you if you're ready to follow your dream of becoming an inspired and successful entrepreneur."

—**Megan Tull**, Owner of Silverlining Concepts, LLC

"Forget about writing a business plan...First, grab yourself a copy of *Ball Gowns to Yoga Pants: Entrepreneurial Secrets to Creating Your Dream Business and Brand*! Dr. Shellie shares the inspiration, experience and practical steps to inspire you to take that big leap to grow your business, confidence, and influence in the marketplace. This brilliant book is a joy to read, filled with inspiring stories and the probing questions and practical advice that set you up for success!"

—**Laurean Kile**, Founder & Visionary of Launch Collective Expo, LLC

"Looking to start your dream business? Dr. Shellie Hipsky provides both practical and inspiring advice for how to start your own entrepreneurial business, whether that's a side hustle or your main thing. This book is about pursuing dreams, while simultaneously dealing with real life. Dr. Hipsky shares success strategies from her personal life experiences, as well as strategies from other highly successful business owners. So, step out of that ball gown, slip into your comfiest yoga pants, and curl up in your favorite chair to read *Ball Gowns to Yoga Pants: Success Secrets for Creating your Dream Business and Brand*. It will change your life!"

—**Laurie Crookell**, CEO of Learning for Life

Ball Gowns to Yoga Pants™

TO YOGA PANTS™

Entrepreneurial Secrets for Creating Your Dream Business and Brand

DR. SHELLIE HIPSKY

NEW YORK

LONDON • NASHVILLE • MELBOURNE • VANCOUVER

Ball Gowns to Yoga Pants™

Entrepreneurial Secrets for Creating Your Dream Business and Brand

Published in New York, New York, by Morgan James Publishing. Morgan James is a trademark of Morgan James, LLC. www.MorganJamesPublishing.com

Although every effort has been made to ensure that the information in this book is correct at the time of going to press, the author has written from her own viewpoint, and therefore, all information is a personal opinion. The author and publisher assume no liability to any party as a result of the contents of this book. The stories in this book are based on the author, researched stories, and the outcomes of other entrepreneur's journeys. Although we have made every reasonable attempt to achieve complete accuracy in the content of this book, we assume no responsibility for errors or omissions in the information. These stories have been shared as examples and inspiration only, and we cannot guarantee you will achieve the same results in your own journey.

ISBN 9781642798401 paperback
ISBN 9781642798418 eBook
Library of Congress Control Number: 2019951247

Cover Design by:
Rachel Lopez
www.r2cdesign.com

Interior Design by:
Chris Treccani
www.3dogcreative.net

Morgan James is a proud partner of Habitat for Humanity Peninsula and Greater Williamsburg. Partners in building since 2006.

Get involved today! Visit
MorganJamesPublishing.com/giving-back

To my parents Dr. and Mrs. Jack and Libby Jacobs, husband Dr. Ken Judson, my amazing kiddos Jacob and Alyssa Hipsky, and of course my incredible Inspiring Lives team (especially my CMO Kelly Frost and my editor Cori Wamsley) for the endless love and support of all my crazy Inspiring Lives projects! Thank you also to Terry Whalin and David Handcock from Morgan James for being patient as I created the very best book for my entrepreneur readers!

TABLE OF CONTENTS

FOREWORD

Dr. Shellie Hipsky left her position as a tenured professor to pursue full-time entrepreneurship and has never looked back. The road as a mompreneur wasn't always easy, as Dr. Shellie will share, but she held steadfast in her decision to conquer her dreams. Because of that, she is now known to the world as the amazing "Dr. Shellie" who is the CEO of Inspiring Lives International, the president of the Global Sisterhood nonprofit, and the editor-in-chief of *Inspiring Lives Magazine*.

Dr. Shellie is the mentor you have been wishing for to figure out how to successfully create, launch, and lead your dream business and brand! She is driven, resilient and compassionate, a woman that has taken life by the horns and gone after her dreams unapologetically.

Over the years, I have had the pleasure of getting to know Dr. Shellie on a personal and professional level. I have witnessed her natural ability to connect women across borders, bring out inspirational stories of women that have overcome significant obstacles, and serve as a pillar of hope to many less fortunate women and children.

I have experienced her emotional impact on audiences as they sit glued to their seats, listening attentively as she interviews women who have entrusted her to share their most vulnerable stories while in talk show studios in Hollywood, in her award-winning *Inspiring Lives Magazine*, and during keynotes internationally. Dr. Shellie's inspiration shines through no matter the platform. She is equally impactful whether dressed in a designer gown and all glammed up delivering a talk on a mega Hollywood stage or in yoga pants at a local women's casual networking event.

When I was invited to write this forward, I was honored. This book is the game changer so many entrepreneurs need. Dr. Shellie is one of the most driven, yet compassionate people I know. She doesn't just wait on opportunities to come her way, she creates them. She doesn't hope that doors will open; she creates entrances so not only she can walk through the door of hope and possibility, but others can follow behind her. If anyone can teach entrepreneurs how to succeed, it would be Dr. Shellie.

You have just made one of the best investments EVER: this book, *Ball Gowns to Yoga Pants™: Entrepreneurial Secrets for Creating Your Dream Business and Brand*! Get ready to go on an educational, impactful, and inspirational ride that will change the entire trajectory of your life and business.

As a practicing entrepreneur who has built several successful businesses, I know firsthand the difficulties facing entrepreneurs embarking upon the entrepreneurial journey. If only I had a blueprint when I started, success would have likely come much sooner. That's why I am excited for you because in this book, Dr. Shellie succinctly lays out the essential steps that can catapult an entrepreneur's career. Information without implementation is useless, which is why I love how Dr. Shellie guides the reader chapter by chapter by first laying out a roadmap of essential strategies and then following up with an assignment requiring stepping into action and implementing that strategy.

I always say, "Success leaves clues." Well you are in for a real treat because you are about to be given Dr. Shellie's entrepreneurial success clues. You will learn the essential steps, strategies, and principles Dr. Shellie used to become an award-winning entrepreneur. Not only that, Dr. Shellie shares lessons from other successful entrepreneurs, many of whom have grown their businesses from zero dollars to millions and/or billions of dollars.

What you are going to love most about this book is that, at the end, you will think, "I can do this," and guess what, if you implement the strategies Dr. Shellie lays out for you, you WILL do this! If you are ready to get the secrets you need to become a successful entrepreneur, implement the techniques, and be inspired along the way, you are in the right place . . . so keep reading this book until the very end.

"Congratulations you are a successful entrepreneur!" I am speaking your success into existence because it is possible for you. Are you excited yet? You should be because, my good friend, the amazing Dr. Shellie Hipsky is your guide for the rest of this journey, and she is going to reveal her entrepreneurial secrets for creating your dream business and brand.

Shevelle McPherson, Esquire

Internationally Acclaimed Business Growth and Legal Strategist, International Bestselling Author and International Speaker

Your *Why* is *Known;* You Need to *Establish* the *HOW!*

INTRODUCTION:

SUCCESS SECRET #1:

Your WHY is Known; You Need to Establish the HOW!

You. Yes, YOU! This is truly TOP SECRET!

I have never really gotten into the nitty gritty details of how I became a successful CEO even though I keep getting asked. Yet, I felt that since this is my 13th book, it was time to teach the future and current entrepreneurs how I got here and how multi-millionaire company leaders got to this level, while helping you create an action plan for your own dream business!

As the boss, when my team comes to me, they need to come armed with a solution, not just the problem. This was a personal policy I made for myself back when I was an employee. I would figure out at least one solution to the issue before I would approach my boss. It is probably one of the reasons that I was able to quickly rise to the top throughout my careers.

I surprised my university colleagues by taking the leap of faith into being the CEO of the motivational media company Inspiring Lives International from my decade-long professor position, which I had attained tenure with. My problem was that I needed to have flexibility of schedule and the ability to grow my company that already had forward momentum plus an audience that was clamoring for more, and I knew that I had the solution for truly empowering and inspiring lives . . . including my own.

This book features my teaching style that earned me the title of "Super Professor" and my CEO savvy that garnered me awards such as "Best Business Woman of the Year" plus "Entrepreneur of the Year." It has been on my heart to help you find the entrepreneurial secrets that you desire and you deserve.

Please dive head first into this book! Mark it up with your unique life experiences, dreams, goals, and action plans, and by the end, you will have your own success secrets. I am cheering for you every step of the way with every page you turn because I genuinely believe that there is a reason you chose this book.

Deep inside, you yearn for the entrepreneurial success secrets. Maybe it's because it drives you nuts that, in a traditional work environment, you don't have the creative freedom or control you desire. Or you can't stand one more day of dropping your child off at daycare and picking them up at night, both when it's dark outside. Maybe you could provide the solution to others' problems through your product or service, while creating wealth for yourself and your family. If you are destined to become an entrepreneur, a point in your life will come when you are working what the world considers to be a "normal job," and you realize it is not serving your greater purpose or giving you the life-balance you deserve.

Whatever your WHY is, we are going to find it. Through ***Ball Gowns to Yoga Pants*™: *Success Secrets for Creating your Dream Business and Brand***, you will also discover your HOW. You are worth it, and it's time that the world benefits from your abilities and expertise!

Just as I encourage my EmpowerU Master Class students— who have had amazing transformations in their careers and lives by engaging in my curriculum—grab a pen, and start reading the stories of my journey. Plus, learn lessons from other top successful entrepreneurs like ***Sara Blakely*** of Spanx and compare your own mission and values to that of Google's "Ten Things We Know to be True." By the end of this book, you will have your own start to your entrepreneurial success story, and I will see you at the top!

Base YOUR
Big Crazy
Idea on
Solving Clients'
Problems

Following Your
While
Passion

CHAPTER ONE:

SUCCESS SECRET #2:

Base YOUR Big Crazy Idea on Solving Clients' Problems While Following Your Passion

"Your work is going to fill a large part of your life, and the only way to be truly satisfied is to do what you believe is great work. And the only way to do great work is to love what you do."
— **STEVE JOBS**, Cofounder, CEO, Chairman Apple Inc.

"Send." I did it! I hit the send button on my resignation email to the university.

No one believed that I would leave a cushy tenured professor position. After all, I had been making 6-figures with benefits and respect that I had worked so hard to earn.

1

Before we go any further, let's examine the pros and cons of jumping into entrepreneurship. Please don't skip this step. Certainly, don't just up and quit a good job without thinking it all through! As a friend once said to me, if you have a stable job that allows you to collect a paycheck and benefits while working your side-hustle, "Ride that bad boy 'til the wheels fall off!"

What would the issues be if you left your stable job for entrepreneurship?

1.

2.

3.

Now that we got that out of the way, what would the benefits of being your own boss and a thriving entrepreneur be?

1.

2.

3.

Let's look at how I became a CEO. I had a rocky start that forced me into being a business woman based on my dream of inspiring the world.

Let me lay it out for you . . . after years of writing academic books based on what I taught my future teachers and leaders from the undergrad to the Ph.D. level, I started writing inspirational books. The real-life stories were so compelling and inspiring that I was drawn toward creating a television show based on them.

All was going full steam ahead with my TV show. I had secured sponsorship for the television show to be produced and distributed, the talk show scripts were created and loaded into the teleprompters, people were hired, the multimillion-dollar NBC-affiliated studio was booked, and the guests were ready to fly in from around the globe to my hometown to film.

My sponsors asked for a lot of voluntary work before the actual check would be cut, though, so I was ready to be the face of a financial institution. They had me do multiple pro-bono speaking keynotes for their leadership teams, and I hosted women-in-business events, attended multiple meetings about our sponsoring partnership, and led videotaped focus groups with respected women from my network. This was all under the understanding that the company was going to be the lead sponsor for my television show.

Days before I was to hand over the big check to the studio, I received a call from the financial sponsor. They had decided that they may not get the return on their investment in the talk show, so they were pulling out *completely* from the sponsorship.

My heart sank. I just had to figure it out. I didn't consider myself to be a business woman, but I knew I had to become one quickly, or my dream wouldn't come to fruition.

I nervously went into my small local bank alone and sat down with the lead business banker. I didn't focus on the sponsor backing out; rather, I started telling her some of the stories of my guests who were going to be on my show and who were in my books. I knew in my heart-of-hearts that I was going to make an impact with the show by truly inspiring lives. After she listened to my story, we both had to wipe away tears that were welling up in our eyes. We both knew that I was going to reach people with my stories and empower lives.

She no longer looked at me as just an education professor with just a lofty idea. Instead, she perceived me as a business woman with a plan, purpose, and passion. She made a few phone calls and secured my first business line of credit. I walked into the studio the next day and presented them with the full check for 13 episodes of my television show *Inspiring Lives with Dr. Shellie*.

I fell into needing startup capital. Take a moment and think through where you could get money to start your business or fund taking it to the next level if you have been operating small.

- Would you be able to "boot strap" and pay for it with money you had saved? If so, how much would you have to work with if you did it now? If you resigned in a year? In two years?
- Would you need a small business loan or line of credit? Check your credit score and see if you could secure funding through a bank.
- Could someone invest in you? Would you utilize an angel investor (a person who provides financial backing for an entrepreneur's startup)? If so, are you willing to surrender some control and a percentage of the profits to an outside investor?

I turned to the bank for capital to start my television show because it was the only valid option I could foresee at the time as a brand-new business person. And it worked! The shows included powerful interviews such as the harrowing story of *Alicia Kozakiewicz*, the first cyber kidnapping survivor, and how her trauma led to preventative safety education, National Child Abuse Awareness Month, and effective legislation to keep others safe. Each episode featured segments like "What's Inspiring You" and "Gratitude Giving" for products that gave back a large percentage to a charity.

The socially conscious programing was globally streamed with an active chat room through a New York City television station that picked up the show. By hosting discussions on important topics ranging from domestic violence to homelessness in real-time, my audience grew. I loved having my TV show. I was interviewing fascinating people who had been through so much, but *Inspiring Lives with Dr. Shellie* really focused on the guest's happy endings. I was telling the stories of people internationally who had conquered their obstacles and gone on to help others.

Then one day, I went to a seminar for women small business owners. We were all sitting at round tables in a hotel banquet room. At this point, some of the audience in the room knew me from my professor position, I was on their TVs weekly, and I was being followed by many on social media. The hostess of the workshop spotted me sitting there and, with a smile, inquired into the mic, "So Dr. Shellie, what's new in your very public and perfect life that we are seeing everywhere lately?"

I burst into tears. (You are probably reading this and thinking I cry an awful lot . . . and you would be right with that assumption, especially during that time of my life.) I had just gotten evidence the day before that I would have to divorce my husband. I explained to the crowd that, yes, my life is public. But it was far from perfect. That I had just realized I needed to get a divorce. Also, that I could no longer do my TV show that I loved, because my life was going to be turned upside down financially and emotionally, and I needed to be there for my children.

Needing to go through a divorce while raising a toddler and a kindergartner, it was so clear that producing a studio show while maintaining a full-time professor position wasn't going to work. I poured myself into parenting and teaching at the university, and all the while, more and more fantastic stories were appearing my life. Stories that I knew needed to be told.

Fortunately, with the guidance of a friend in the media world, I changed my platform to Empowering Women Radio. I was syndicated to over 120 radio stations internationally. I was able to tape from my own home on my own time after my kids were asleep at night and then edit and send out to the radio stations.

Real life happens when we are building a business. And my divorce altered the way I presented my content and ran my company.

- **What personal life challenges have you been faced with lately that could impact your business in the future? From health issues to relationship insecurities, take a moment to think how these could affect you.**
- **Speaking of relationships, how would it affect your partner, aging parents, spouse, and/or children (if you have them) if you were to leave your current position to pursue building a company? For example, are they counting on you providing the health insurance for your family?**

Once I had started the divorce process and custody was being smoothed out, I was able to form some great friendships with the women I interviewed for my radio show. I saw a book emerging from the stories that were being told to me and my radio listeners. I started to see that there were common threads between the stories. I earned a sabbatical from the university, and I dove into writing the book *Common Threads* based on my radio interviews.

One night, as I was analyzing the tremendous amount of transcripts (over a thousand pages worth in binder), I was struck with a desperate need to paint. I went to my 5-year-old daughter's art easel that my father had built for her, and I grabbed her paint brushes and primary colors.

Lacking a canvas, I pulled a sheet from my linen closet. I was compelled to boldly paint in three different styles and colors the words "INSPIRATION," "EMPOWERMENT," and "BALANCE." I stared at the words. Not knowing yet what they meant to me, I cut holes in the top folded and sewn part of the sheet. Then, I stood on a chair and pulled down the curtain in my bedroom. I threaded the sheet with the words facing me so I could see them on the curtain rod.

Thank goodness I was newly single, because I am sure that a life-mate would have been so confused by the scribbled words hung over the big window!

I stared at the sheet with my arms folded and a confused scowl on my face. Finally, one-word sprung to my mind . . .

"Trilogy!"

I needed to create three books based on the 100 top interviews from my Empowering Women Radio show: *Inspiration*, *Empowerment*, and *Balance*.

As the books were taking shape, I interviewed **Wendy Lydon**, an awesome business coach, for Empowering Women Radio. I remember planning out my life from personal to business goals with her. Then, she had me talk about them and rank my urgency. And she said to me, "The one dream that you keep bringing up is that you have always wanted to go to Paris. Why can't you make that a reality?" A month later, I was told by my friend about an incredible yoga and writing retreat in Paris. I decided it was time for me to make it happen.

I booked the Parisian trip, and off I flew during my sabbatical. Writing in quaint cafes. Meditation and yoga with powerful women. Group writing with intriguing prompts in French rose gardens and at the base of the Eiffel Tower. It was exactly what I needed to breathe life into my book series.

At that time in my life, I needed to make my Paris dream come true. It wasn't until I wrote down what I needed in all areas of my life that I realized how important this dream had been to me since I was a young girl. I actually recall being an elementary-aged child and filling my pockets with quarters. I grabbed a large wide-brimmed hat with black sequins and tulle from my mother's costume closet (she ran the local theater and had fabulous dress up pieces). I walked all the way to the local deli, Lou and Hy's. I was seated at a table by a confused hostess who probably thought I looked ridiculous: a child wearing a Kermit the Frog t-shirt, corduroy pants, and a gigantic black hat.

In my mind, though, I was not in a deli in Akron, Ohio. I was transported to a Parisian café, and I was ordering my delicious cup of tea with sugar. In my imagination, I was having the adventure of a lifetime, and I looked so sophisticated to all who saw this mysterious young lady in the black hat. I had envisioned my Paris writing adventure decades before I ever got to really experience it!

After I was able to truly journey to Paris and create *real* memories, I was delighted with the richness of the experience. My senses seemed heightened, and my writing was improving as I told the women's stories in the books.

I was able to follow my heart's desires, which led me down a winding alley to a vintage Parisian boutique. I found a 1950s couture gown that I modeled in front of the Eiffel Tower for the cover of the first book in the series, titled *Common Threads: Inspiration*. It was a girlie dream-come-true for me. And this experience foreshadowed modeling in my future as Inspiring Lives evolved.

Let's look at what experiences *you* desire. To open your mind to the possibilities, let's look at what your dreams are.

- **What experience is on your "bucket list" that you *must* find a way to make happen?**
- **Would your current job allow you to attain those dreams on your bucket list? If not, is there a side-hustle or job that would be better suited for you to check off your bucket list? (For example, in the book *Big Magic*, Elizabeth Gilbert talked about waitressing and bartending jobs that allowed her to write, travel, and not take job pressures home with her.)**
- **If you had your dream life and you could travel anywhere and have any experience, what would it be?**

I returned to my Pittsburgh home from my Paris yoga and writing retreat with renewed energy. I had a burning passion for more travel, though, so I knew it would be difficult to return to the monotony of teaching the same lesson plans over and over for a decade after my sabbatical. Not to mention following the administration's strict office hours rules. Or being discouraged from forming friendships with my students. That was especially tough because I was forming mentoring bonds with them and was clearly making a profound difference. These things started to weigh heavily on me. I could imagine what I could do with the freedom to really take my little Inspiring Lives, LLC to the next level and make it Inspiring Lives International.

Then, when I interviewed **Kate Batten** out of the United Kingdom, who recorded the15 Minute Motivation podcast, she told me that she was planning a women's retreat and that all the ladies would be in a pin-up calendar. I was so in! My dear friend Beth Shari, who is a costume designer and vintage clothing expert, and I headed to the beaches in California for this trip.

During a group circle beachside discussion, we all said what we would do if we had no limits. I exclaimed aloud for the first time, "I will quit my tenured professor job. I will make my book series a bestseller. And I will make my company Inspiring Lives International a huge success around the world!" And wow did I ever!

- **What would you do to become successful if you had no limits?**
- **What noise in your head is holding you back from trying to reach that limitless dream?**

Right after I made that claim to the women about what I would do with no limits, I couldn't believe it came out of my mouth, and with people I barely knew listening to me. I thought, "My parents would be so disappointed if I quit after I worked so hard to earn tenure. What if the books don't sell? What if I am never a real business woman . . . if I am just 'faking it until I make it,' forever?"

- **Do you have "imposter syndrome," which makes you feel like you will be discovered as a fraud? Like you are not a true business person, and you will be found out? If so, take a moment, and write down your deepest fear about this.**

- **Now, take that fear (such as "I am not a real business woman, and they will find out!"), and rewrite it for yourself in reverse so you can see it in black and white: "People will find out that I am a real business woman, and they will want to work with me!" Type or write this phrase somewhere where you will be able to see it because you are not an imposter. You, my friend, are the real deal!**

I did go back to being a university professor after my sabbatical, but not for long. While I loved the students, my Inspiring Lives International company was growing. Universities and companies around the world were requesting me to keynote and inspire their audiences. And I was getting married to an amazing man who was very supportive of me pursuing my dream career while raising my children. My three books were launched as *Common Threads*, the trilogy in *Inspiration*, *Empowerment*, and *Balance*. All three books made the Amazon International Bestseller List at the same time! My life had turned around, and I was ready to make the leap of faith into entrepreneurship full time.

My big crazy idea was that I would be inspiring lives internationally through a motivational media company. Let's start brainstorming YOUR big crazy idea! First, evaluate whether it would be smarter for you to simply buy into a franchise or do network marketing with a ready-made business that is already pre-branded and established as a business entity. You can still use this book to enhance that business and yourself leading it, but if you need to discover your unique idea and make a business from that idea . . . I can't wait to watch you blossom into a successful entrepreneur!

- **What are you truly passionate about?**
- **What would your ideal business be based on? What are your skills? Your purpose?**

To have a business, you need to create demand. And to get the demand for your product or service, you need to solve a problem for your customer.

- **What problem do you want to solve for people?**
- **Brain dump all the ideas for a business that you would like to create.**
- **Write out a one-sentence description of what you would like your business to be.**
- **What will you name your company? (Pro-tip: Make sure that you trademark it and legally create a corporation with your name).**

Now that you have your basic concept and a name for your company, you are well on your way to bringing your dreams to fruition, to being your own boss!

Everyone *Defines* Success Differently & Your *Vision*/Mission Must be *Crystal Clear.*

CHAPTER TWO:

SUCCESS SECRET #3:

Everyone Defines Success Differently and Your Vision/Mission Must be Crystal Clear

"An Entrepreneur is someone who has a vision for something and a want to create."
— **DAVID KARP**, Founder and CEO of Tumblr

"I want to inspire, educate, entertain, and empower the world." It was written in my handwriting on a tattered pink notecard taped to the corner of my mirror. That simple sentence became a motto and almost a battle cry for me since I wrote it down over a decade ago. It is also the foundation of my personal mission/vision statements. While I was creating and building my company and nonprofit, I always referred to that sentence to ensure that I stayed on track. This chapter will help you determine what your mission and visions are for your company.

The "why" for your business is your mission statement. The vision is "what" you will be doing. The rest of this book will help you determine "how" to become a successful entrepreneur. Plus, you will learn so much from being in the trenches of truly running a business!

Right now, enjoy a little you time. Some quiet time. Pour yourself a glass of wine or a cup of tea, sit down at your computer or grab a pen and paper, and just be with yourself.

You are going to lead this company, but before you do that, we need to examine what you are aiming for. We need to know what success looks like for you, because unless you know what it *truly* is, you're never going to hit those milestones. You're never going to take that action, if you don't know where you're going.

You don't go on a road trip without first plugging your destination into your GPS because you need to know how to get there. And if you don't know where you're going in life and your career, you're never going to get where you would like to be.

- **Define success. Success to me is** _____ _____.

- **I will know that I am successful when I have these three things:**
   1.

2.

3.

I love vision boarding. I'm not sure if you have a vision board already, but by the time you're done reading this, you will want to get your magazines, poster board, and scissors, or print things out from the computer, and start to collage your dreams.

Maybe there was a time when you really wanted to add a special person to your life, so you were putting it out into the universe that you needed that special person. If you had put it on a vision board, the Law of Attraction would have helped you attract them faster because whatever you put out in the universe comes back to you. I discovered that this is true when my young daughter wrote a checklist of what she wanted in a new life partner for me. It wasn't a vision board, but it worked the same way.

I went through a tricky divorce. I was a single mom. My daughter Alyssa was 8 years old, precocious, and absolutely adorable when she came to me with a 50-item list of what she needed and what I needed in an "extra dad" figure in her life.

It was absolutely amazing to me that I then found that person a few months later because it was specific enough and my heart was ready for this type of love. Alyssa was so specific in her requirements, down to the idea that he had to have a dog, love to read books, and be a very hard worker. Her list put the idea out in the universe that this is what I needed, and I found my "Mr. Ken"—Dr. Ken Judson—through Match.com because I was so specific. My kids and even my social media friends and Inspiring Lives team still refer to him as "Mr. Ken" because that's how he was introduced to my children.

After meeting him, I thought I would wait six months to let him meet my kiddos (because I needed to be sure he was the one), but during the last month of that waiting period, he helped my brother, who was visiting from Colorado, and my father build a beautiful Colonial-style wooden two-story playhouse. I could see that not only was he the hard worker I needed, but he was also becoming part of my family. It was clear that they all loved him.

I had the vision for the type of relationship I needed. I knew what I was looking for, and—this is hugely important—I took action! You need to establish a vision for yourself, relationships, and of course, your company. Taking massive action and getting buy-in from your team once you have one is important.

I interviewed *John Assaraf*, the CEO of three multimillion-dollar companies and teacher of *The Secret* in Rhonda Byrne's book and the movie, on my Facebook talk show Inspiring Lives LIVE! Assaraf taught my audience how to use Innercise to train their brains for what they desired. He also explained that *The Secret* didn't quite get it right because it made people think that you could just wish for something and it would just happen. Making the vision clear is important, but the action steps beyond that are vital. You have to put in the work to make your vision a reality.

Over the years, my vision boards have definitely changed. At times I have divided mine up into four quadrants: financial, relationships, travel, and inner peace, for example. You can use whatever is aesthetically pleasing to you.

As you are skimming through your magazine collection and creating your vision board, I want you to pick the right things, the things that really jump out to you, that really say something to you and to your heart, to your future business, to who you are as a professional, and who you want to become, because that's what's going to come to you.

Nobody wants to feel stagnant. No one wants to just repeat the same thing over-and-over again. We all have goals that are nibbling at us, and you have to figure out how to make them happen, how you can take action on them. To do this, you need to be able to see them. I implore you right now to get your magazines, get your big poster boards, get your glue sticks, get your tape, and do it.

I even got my daughter to create vision boards, and we do it side-by-side. It's that important!

One woman who always comes to mind is the vision board queen, who wrote *The Big Ask*, **Lucinda Cross**. I was able to interview her in New York City. She has been on *The Today Show*, explaining to America and the world how to vision board. But long before that moment, her life wasn't always easy. It wasn't always good. Her incredibly powerful, inspiring story starts with going to federal prison at 19-years-old. She then harnessed the power of vision boarding to not only get herself out of that pit, but to rise higher than anyone ever thought she would rise. Now, she teaches women around the world how to make this happen in their own lives.

The people who I have suggested vision boarding to have made huge things happen. The women and men who didn't do it, though, are still sitting there, every time I see them, complaining that they're still not getting their dreams. I always say, "Oh, honey, that is rough," but I also think, "Do your homework."

If somebody tells you to try what they did to accomplish what you are striving for, listen to them, follow their path, take them on as a mentor, and I'm telling you right now—GET VISION BOARDING!

When I interviewed **Caryn Chow**, CEO of Calyx Concierge in New York City, for Empowering Women Radio, my then-assistant Brittany was sitting across the room from me. Brittany was at a very different point in her life than she is now. She was young, a single mom to a beautiful daughter. She was figuring out the world and doing everything she could to become who she thought she could be. So she was listening intently during the interview. We were talking about manifesting things in your life, taking a chance, and making things happen for yourself.

A few months later, Brittany and I traveled to the Hollywood area and stayed in a very swanky hotel to do media work. We had a lot of fun, and we did many interviews with superstar inspiring ladies. It was during the time of the Oscars, and it was fantastic. We rented a Corvette and drove around.

That night, she told me that she had set up a date with a guy in the area who she was friends with from college, so I said, "Why don't you take the Corvette?" And she did. The next time I saw her, she was just glowing, and we started talking more about what had happened with Chow and manifesting her dream life.

Today, Brittany is no longer my assistant. Instead, she is living in the Hollywood/LA area with this incredible man, who she took the Corvette to meet that night. She had used all of Chow's manifesting tips, and they are now married.

Her sweet daughter got a daddy, and they recently welcomed a precious baby boy into their family. Theirs is a true and lovely testimony about what can manifest when you put things out into the universe using the Law of Attraction. Utilize your strengths, and put your desires on a vision board. Wonderful things will come back to you in your personal and professional life.

Visions and missions can start on the vision board, but they should be refined into clear statements for your team and clients. Let's look at the visions/missions of other respected entrepreneurs garnered from their company's websites.

Bethenny Frankel, like many other entrepreneurs of our time, really made a name for herself by being cast in reality shows, from Bravo's *Real Housewives of New York* to *The Apprentice: Martha Stewart.* She used the shows as a platform to show the world her SkinnyGirl® brand, while branding herself in the process. Before that, she started off her entrepreneurial life buying cashmere pashmina scarves inexpensively and selling them to her posh friends. She got very good at marketing and wound up selling her SkinnyGirl Cocktails for a reported $100 million.

Frankel believes that not only do companies need mission statements, but those who run them need personal mission statements as well. She wrote for *Glamour* that her mission was to support herself on her own terms. She said that she told herself, "You are destined for something special. But no one can do it for you, and no one can save you. You have to save yourself."[1] She had many failed relationships and talked about her dysfunctional family on TV (even in broadcast therapy sessions) and in writing. As a mompreneur of a daughter, she knew that building her life on her terms was important not only to model a behavior that would help her daughter succeed but also to provide the kind of life that she wanted for them both.

She has talked about her savvy for business and for creating a life she loves as a *Shark Tank* TV guest judge, on her former talk show *Bethenny* (which was executive produced by Ellen DeGeneres), and in one of her *New York Times* bestselling books *A Place of Yes: Ten Rules for Getting Everything You Want Out of Life*. Many women flock to see Frankel speak publicly because she is relatable, crass but classy, and uses humor to tell a story.

Let's look at what your personal and business mission statements should be:

- **What would your personal mission statement say?**
- **How would your personal mission vary from what your business mission statement would be?**

Joanna Gaines and her husband *Chip Gaines* began their Magnolia lifestyle brand with a small family-run home goods shop called Magnolia Market in 2003. While the shop has since closed so they could focus on their growing family, the Magnolia Homes construction business functioned under the mission of "making Waco, Texas, beautiful one home at a time."[2]

As the stars of HGTV's *Fixer Upper*, they were the couple that made audiences giggle at Chip's antics while he did amazing DIY work. Viewers admired Joanna's beautiful, simple, and charming interior aesthetic.

While the mission for their construction company was very specific to a niche area in Texas, their bigger company Magnolia Homes' includes a glossy magazine, home goods that are sold in multiple retail markets, stylized rental properties, a bakery, and more. For all these endeavors, they went beyond a mission statement and created the Magnolia Manifesto, "Of all heroic pursuits large or small, we believe that there may be none greater than a life well loved." A manifesto is a public declaration of motives, views, or intentions. It states core values and truths.

- **What do you believe for sure about what you want to achieve?**
- **What are your core values?**
- **What would your manifesto be?**

Rachel Hollis is the mother of four and successful event planner who built up The Chic Site teaching readers everything from recipes to fashion and style tips. She's also the *New York Times* bestselling author of *Girl, Wash Your Face*. Recently, she stated that her company motto for years has been "Giving women the tools to change their lives."[3]

Fourteen years after founding her company, Hollis decided to hire her husband on as the CEO because she realized that when she made a list of the things that she loved to do for the company, none of them fell under that job description. As you are planning your company—or many years later—you may decide that you love being the face of the company and doing the creative work, so the operations should be handled by another person.

- **What tasks and jobs do you really look forward to with your company?**
- **Which tasks and jobs could you delegate?**

When Hollis and her husband changed the name of their company to Hollis Co., together they decided that they would no longer commit to any new business that didn't fit into their company's goals just because it was a financial opportunity. She, like other lifestyle influencers, was getting product promotion offers constantly. When they moved forward with the company, they decided they would only focus energy on things that help their audience change their lives for the better.

- **What will you not compromise on with your company when it comes to following your vision?**
- **What is your deeper mission that you will not sell out or waiver from as the company leader?**

You need to focus on your own mission. Don't get distracted by things that don't fit what you are all about at your core. You don't want to confuse your audience, water down your brand, or turn off future customers because they can't figure out what you are really all about. A perfect example of a focused business leader is the cookie queen, Debbi Fields.

Debbi Fields, the founder of Mrs. Fields Original Cookies, was told that she was crazy for trying to start a store that only sold cookies in 1977! Her father only made $15,000 per year as a welder for the United States Navy, and he provided for a family of six. According to Fields, "My father believed that true wealth was found in family, friends, and doing what you love."[4]

Her siblings didn't like food made with imitation products, which was all they could afford. So, at age 13, Fields started working in a department store, and her first paycheck went toward real eggs, sugar, and butter for a special treat: cookies.

She started with a single cookie recipe of her design. Eventually, she became a multimillionaire with her chain of cookie and baked goods stores. Her mission has always been "To create the highest quality product possible—every time." She started with a tiny kitchen as a teenager, and now through her worldwide franchise, she is known for both sweetness and success.

- **Will quality be a part of your mission? If so, with your product or service, how will you determine that it is of the highest quality that you can provide to your customers?**
- **What is your niche? You need to determine what you will be focused on providing for your customers.**

World-renowned dermatologists *Dr. Katie Rodan* and *Dr. Kathy Fields* started in 2002 with a department store brand based on clinical results, and now they have a billion-dollar product sold by over 150,000 independent consultants. Both

Drs. Rodan and Fields have hit the "Forbes' List of America's Richest Self Made Women" and have an estimated net worth of $550 million. Their mission is, "At the core of everything we do is a commitment to create positive change in people's skin, in their lives, and ultimately, in the lives of others."[5]

- **What change do you want to make in people's lives with your product or service?**
- **If you envision someday franchising or doing network marketing with your product, how would this serve your greater mission?**

Angie Hicks realized that word of mouth advertising for contractors could be done online in a database, so she created "Angie's List" and became a millionaire. It started with a real problem when she was an intern for a venture capitalist, and he needed to find a reliable contractor. When she realized the need for a services referral business, Hicks went door-to-door in Columbus, Ohio, asking about contractor referrals. Now, millions of people use Angie's List to find just the right housekeepers, painters, landscapers, electricians, and more. What started out as a call-in service to determine which contractors should be hired became a multimillion-dollar business that utilizes an online database to match people with recommended providers.[6]

- **How could you utilize the internet to provide value for your customers?**

- **How can your company's mission be enhanced with automation so you aren't working constantly but are still providing the quality service that your customers deserve?**

Now, you have defined your version of success, vision boarded, and looked at other successful entrepreneurs and how they achieved value-based multimillion-dollar companies. Look back at everything you have written down or cut out. Look for themes and draft your mission and vision statements for your company.

- **Examine why your business will provide the product or service. What is your company's mission statement?**
- **Focusing on what your company will do for its clients. What is your company's vision statement?**

By forming mission and vision statements, you will be better prepared to lead your company and communicate your vision to funders, customers, and your team. Remember that with time, leadership, and staff input, the statement may morph, yet the core values that you establish in the beginning will almost always stay the same.

It's Not Just
Who & What
You *Know;*
— It's WHO —
Trusts, Respects,
& *Relates*
to
YOU

CHAPTER THREE

SUCCESS SECRET #4:

It's Not Just Who You Know and What You Know; It's WHO Trusts, Respects, and Relates to You

"Networking has been cited as the number one unwritten rule of success in business. Who you know really impacts what you know."
— **SALLIE KRAWCHECK**, CEO Ellevest and Former President of the Global Wealth & Investments Management division of Bank of America

Networking is so vital for business owners. If people don't know about you, your company, products, and/or services, how in the world can they purchase from you? It is vital to be connected to people. Some people, like me, have what I refer to as a "brain rolodex" that they use to connect the right people, causing a powerful chain reaction of networking and relationship.

I want to tell you a story of when I first realized that I was a true connector. It all started very dramatically when I bellowed . . .

"We are going to die this way!"

I screamed this phrase as the white Jeep tipped on the mountain cliff in Costa Rica. The downpour was beating heavily on the rental car's roof. My father couldn't see to drive through the curtain of water, and mudslides were forming next to the car.

The GPS was no longer working, and we were completely lost. I was terrified and just praying that we would survive the night.

It was Christmas Eve, and the "Original Four," as we call ourselves (my mom who I call "Moo," my dad, my brother John, and I) were on a family vacation. My brother, who speaks fluent Spanish, thought that we could go off the beaten path. However, we found ourselves in a dangerous situation, and I couldn't help but think that we were going to die together as a family.

As night came, the rain just kept falling on the muddy roads. I tried to make conversation with my brother. I referenced the book that I was reading as we set out earlier in the Jeep. Through my fear, I started talking to him about *Malcolm Gladwell*'s *Tipping Point* to distract us from the terror I was experiencing. Gladwell says that there are three different types of people: the mavens, the salespeople, and the connectors.[7]

Mavens are information people who are always in the know. They deal in information, processes, and systems. **Salespeople** are those who are persuasive and are all about the sizzle of a project. **Connectors** are the people people with the internal rolodexes who have the gift to connect people from everywhere to make a powerful impact on their lives.

As we were distracting ourselves from the tropical storm, we realized that my brother and I were clearly both connectors according to Gladwell's theory. Whereas others may feel that the world was so big, John and I have always been able to connect others internationally through friendships. When we meet a new friend, we immediately focus on their skills and what they might offer to others.

Just as we finally got our mind off of what I thought was impending doom (our inevitable deaths on Christmas Eve in the rainforest) . . . A man appeared in the distance.

He was dressed in a black tuxedo and holding an ebony umbrella. I rubbed my eyes, thinking this must be some type of mirage.

We confirmed, as a family, that this was really happening, and my dad slid the car to a halt. The dapper gentleman opened the car doors and said "Welcome to the Peace Lodge." Much to our disbelief we had magically stumbled upon a 5-star hotel in Costa Rica on Christmas Eve, and they actually had room at the inn! We would not die that evening. We laughed heartily as we each drank a bottle of red wine and devoured gourmet food in one of the incredible restaurants the Peace Lodge offered.

The following days were filled with what my brother and I deemed as "'splorin'" as children (which meant "exploring new places"). We got to feed sweet nectar to dozens of hummingbirds, sit covered in butterflies, and zip line through the rainforest. The memories of the Peace Lodge will forever be engrained in these

"Connectors'" minds. And because of my love for storytelling, as evidenced in this true story from years ago, I am truly a Connector-Salesperson because I not only am a people person, but I also adore telling a good tale while persuading others to understand where I am coming from.

- **According to Malcom Gladwell's *Tipping Point* theory, are you a Maven, Salesperson, or a Connector? Are you a combination, and if so, which two do you lean toward the most heavily?**
- **A business really needs all these *Tipping Point* personality types to get to the top of their game. Which of the three should you be on the look-out for while networking to help build your company?**

Networking is so vital for the right customers, clients, team, and supporters when you own a business. As **Robert Kiyosaki** from *Rich Dad, Poor Dad* says, "The richest people in the world look for and build networks, everyone else looks for work."[8]

Let's take a moment and evaluate your current network. Let's start with family and friends. Think about how they will be as a support system for you as you start your business.

Have you ever tried to go on a diet and your loved ones still offered you pizza and their delicious homemade cookies? It can feel like the people who care about you are trying to sabotage you before you even get off the ground. This happens with diets and also with entrepreneurship.

Remember that your significant other may have to experience a lifestyle change through adding daycare, losing health insurance, less money coming in for a while, boot strapping, or change in credit status with loans. And it seems that everyone's mom has an opinion. "Go get a real job. This will never work," can be heard from family and friends.

You must remember that not everyone in your life is going to understand what you are doing. Not all people are cut out to be entrepreneurs. Most people prefer the safety and comfort of a job that pays them steadily where the buck doesn't stop with them and they have benefits and very little risk.

There comes a time when you have to look within for strength. Make sure you have a network besides your family and friends that understands the ups and downs and needs of an entrepreneur.

You may find that awkward competition develops with people in the same industry you are entering with your entrepreneurial venture if you knew those people before.

Anita Brattina is the CEO of Power Link, which forms boards for companies with strategic positions in legal, accounting, marketing, and more to help the business go to the next level. I have been learning a great deal by attending a non-competitive peer group CEO Circle led by Brattina who started as an entrepreneur with a desk in the spare bedroom of her apartment. She went on to build a multimillion-dollar international marketing consulting business.

Brattina and I discussed how truly unusual it is for a person to not only take the entrepreneurial leap of faith but then to grow from local to regional, then national and even international while turning a profit. It takes time, planning, being in the right place at the right time, and networking. That's where groups such as CEO circles, chambers of commerce, and other professional groups can really help you find your tribe.

You need to build your support network through connections. Through mastermind groups, you can form long-lasting business relationships and friendships and find accountability partners. My EmpowerU Master Class cohorts become great network builders for the women involved while they are learning through a proven life transformation curriculum. They learn how to find inspiration, empowerment, and balance, while creating their dream lives and careers. The relationships that are formed during courses and masterminds can really help take you and your business to the next level.

Finding a mentor can also be the ticket to a wonderful sounding board and way to help garner support. **Dr. Claudia Armani-Bavaro** approached me to mentor her before she had her Ph.D. She was a student in the Instructional Management and Leadership program I taught at Robert Morris University in Pittsburgh, Pa. She said that she had always wanted to write a book, and she asked me to write one with her after she heard my lecture "Publish or Perish from Query Letter to Book" during her doctoral course. I suggested that she first finish her coursework, write her dissertation, and successfully defend it in front of her committee to become a doctor. I assured her that we would meet soon as fellow doctors at a coffee house and plot out our book. That's exactly what we did as we co-wrote *Mentoring Magic: Pick the Card for your Success,* together.

While I was mentoring her through the process of writing her first book, I realized how the very best mentoring relationships are truly reciprocal. When I thought back to being mentored and mentoring others over the years, I noticed that the most impactful mentoring relationships included learning and growth for both the mentor and the mentee. I suggest finding a mentor who is willing to guide you, who has walked a similar path to what you desire in your life. The person should be open to and excited about helping lead you through your growth to the next level.

- **Who do you respect who you could approach about mentoring you in your business?**
- **What do you bring to the mentorship table? For example, I have seen younger mentees support their mentor's social media understanding while the mentors help them move in the right circles for their business to take off and thrive.**
- **Research Time: Which local, regional, national, and international professional organizations can help you network and find the right connections for business relationships in your area of expertise?**

Remember that tons of chambers of commerce, professional organizations, networking groups, masterminds, and gatherings are available to choose from, but you don't have to try them all at once. Don't spread yourself too thin. The point is to find your people—your tribe—not just a lot of random people that happen to be in business.

When you are networking, don't feel pressured to make a sale with those you are meeting. Focus on building relationships.

The sales will come because you will attract the right people into your inner circle.

Those in your tribe will get to know you and, most likely, will grow to love your product or service. These relationships can become walking billboards for you as they respect you and what you bring to the table. Testimonials can be your best advertisement for your company, and they can be included in your website, social media, and marketing materials.

- **Which networking groups or professional organizations have you decided you will join?**
- **Who do you already have in your tribe who could attest to your skills, talents, and/or what your business is about?**

When you attend networking gatherings, be sure that it is not just about the exchange of business cards. Rather, it should be an exchange of value. You never know if you could be meeting a future investor, customer, or even a business partner. I always greatly appreciate when I go to these events and, instead of launching into an elevator pitch, the person chatting with me asks how they can support me in Inspiring Lives because they know my company.

Today, there is no reason to go blindly into a room full of business people wearing name tags. Many, many years ago, I went to a job fair when I had just gotten my first degree. I was armed with my resume, reference letters, and a portfolio, but what got me multiple job offers was ingenuity.

I attended the job fair with a college friend, and we both wanted to work in different areas of the country. When I saw the recruiters' faces light up when people had inside knowledge about the jobs they were applying for, I grabbed my friend and pulled her behind a booth. I quickly formulated a plan of attack for the area I wanted to work in and vice versa.

The one who didn't want the job in that location would go up to the booth first and grab the information. They would talk to them for a bit about what they were seeking in a job candidate and about the organization. Then we met at the back of the convention center and gave each other notes on what they were seeking.

I was able to confidently walk up and talk to the job recruiters about positions I wanted, peppering my comments with knowledge about their company and parts of my background that would fit what they desired in a new hire. And BAM! I had many job offers right after college because I knew what they wanted.

Today, it is almost too easy to get information. If you are at a large networking event, you might see a name tag with a job title that sounds like you would be able to work with them to get to your goals. If you aren't particularly savvy at just striking up conversations with strangers, it would be so easy to simply Google the person's bio and or company to know what you have in common, what their company's mission/vision is, and/or some other random tidbit of knowledge.

Remember that, in networking, it's the friendships and authentic relationships that really make an impact on your career. So, listen. Also, ask questions that aren't work-related such as:

- **What are you passionate about?**
- **What restaurant is your favorite in town?**
- **What do you like to do when you aren't working?**

Interact with the person, listen, and by all means, please follow up. Some people network all the time and have a drawer filled with business cards with people that they never connect with. Follow up through social media such as LinkedIn or an email to get to know the person. If there is a strong business connection that you want to cultivate, invite them to your office or out for coffee for further conversation.

Now as you are cultivating your network, you will be bolstered to withstand the naysayers in your life from the beginning. You *are* cut out for the entrepreneur life. Once the people in your world see what you are capable of, most will come around and be very proud of you. However, finding a tribe of business colleagues who can support and celebrate you is a beautiful thing in an entrepreneur's world.

Being
Authentic
— in Your —
Leadership &
Marketing
will —
Attract
the right clients
& *Customers*

BALL GOWNS TO YOGA PANTS

CHAPTER FOUR:

SUCCESS SECRET #5:

Being Authentic in Your Leadership and Marketing will Attract the Right Customers and Clients

"All of us need to understand the importance of branding. We are CEOs of our own companies: Me, Inc. To be in business today, our most important job is to be head marketer for the brand called You."
—TOM PETERS *in* **Fast Company**

"Who does she think she is?" He had no idea that I was within earshot. I was all glammed up in a gown for the American Heart Association Go Red Campaign fashion show. I was, of course, rocking my signature Christian Louboutin high heels with red soles. I had been running around with my photographer getting pictures of people who were giving funds for heart health awareness for the Society Spotlight section of the magazine.

I started to get fired up as he continued talking about me just a few steps away. "I mean, she's on every cover of *Inspiring Lives Magazine*. Does she think she is Oprah? She's a motivational speaker as well, I hear. Does she assume she will be the next Tony Robbins? Seriously, who does she think she is?"

One deep breath later, I tapped on the shoulder of his suit. I flashed him a big smile and stated, "Hi, I am Dr. Shellie Hipsky the CEO of Inspiring Lives International. And no, I don't think I am Oprah or Tony Robbins. I am Dr. Shellie Hipsky. Every day, I just strive to be the best version of myself that I can be."

His mouth dropped open. My friend he was speaking with grinned at me.

The three of us ended up having a great conversation about self-branding. That very evening, I received messages on my phone that he had started following me on Twitter (@DrShellieHipsky) and Instagram (@Dr.Shellie). Later, he became a big supporter of my brand and my magazine. I had stood up for myself, and my personal brand. Through that exchange, I gained a follower and the respect of a man who had pre-judged me.

You may be embarking on your own self-branding journey, or you may be a seasoned pro. Either way, you must begin with yourself. To sell your brand, product, or service, you must have a true grasp of who you are at your core. This book will help you hone in on your personal brand. You will, no doubt, engage in some self-discovery along the way. I encourage you not to copy anyone else's brand. Simply strive to be the best version of yourself, daily . . . and brand accordingly.

Big companies used to be the only ones with "brands." Now, any entrepreneur who is building a business, people seeking employment, or even those who are simply existing in a busy media-filled world, need to consider branding.

As the editor-in-chief of *Inspiring Lives Magazine*, I know first-hand that people want to get to know personalities. People are intrigued by the story of the person behind the brand and are influenced by the heart of the owner, CEO, etc., rather than simply buying based on a catchy slogan or product jingles, like in the past.

As I always say as I sign off from my TV show *Inspiring Lives with Dr. Shellie* and my Facebook talk show Inspiring Lives LIVE, "Inspiration is just a story away." It is up to you to craft your story, and therefore your brand, so it sells and attracts your perfect clients and customers.

Because it is your brand, and not mine, I want you to really think through how you perceive yourself and think about how you want the world to view you.

As Socrates once said, "To know thyself is the beginning of wisdom." To be smart about branding, you need to really know who you are, what you stand for, and what about you is memorable.

If you don't truly know who you are, how can you expect people on social media and potential clients to know you or buy from you? Let's take you way back to begin this self-discovery process. When I was a child, I used to tell anyone who would listen that I wanted to be a happy teacher, a mother, and a performer on Broadway when I grew up. Now I entertain through multiple media forms, and I still belt out songs to help raise funds for charity galas. I am also a mother of two beautiful children. I was a tenured professor at a university training future teachers and leaders for a decade. I think I came close to the mark and my childhood ideas certainly showed hints of what I would be doing now with my life.

Unless you are Peter Pan and refuse to ever grow up, it's likely that you had a vision for your future as a child. Let's look at what you wanted to be.

- **When you were younger, what did you want to be when you grew up?**
- **Is there any connection between what you dreamed you would become and who you are in your daily life?**
- **What held you back from this dream? (For example, my friend said that she never took the leap as an artist because her mother constantly told her that she could never support herself on the money that she would make.)**
- **While you will probably not materialize a job as an astronaut at this point if you are not already one, is there something that you left behind from your early vision of your future self that you could and should reclaim?**

Maybe it was as simple as a vibe or feeling that you wanted or now want to have. Some of us just truly want to experience joy or stability in life. Perhaps you are too stressed all the time, worrying about money, and you always thought you would be a laid back, chilled out person. Or you would like to be considered glamorous, but you can't recall the last time you got dressed up or even out of your yoga pants.

- **Describe the vibe that you are presenting to the world currently.**
- **What vibe would you like to project (maybe you just want to be seen as high-energy and a positive person who brightens up a room)?**

When doing this self-analysis, it may help to talk with your best friend, business partner, or life partner. Or if you already have an active social media group, you could raise some of these questions there so everyone could weigh in about current perceptions. Of course, you are the only one who determines who you are. You just may be surprised by how you are being perceived by others.

When I was a professor at a private university making a salary and earning my tenure promotion, it was easy to say what I did for a living. Entrepreneurs, though, may not have a job that is easy to explain.

We need to define to ourselves what we do as empowered entrepreneurs so we can explain it to others . . . although, your parents may never really grasp what it is that you do or see it as a "real job." Let's look at what you do and who you do it for.

- **Describe the main service or product that you provide for clients.**

- **Write down your concept of the perfect client or customer, being as specific as you can. For example, *Inspiring Lives Magazine*'s ideal subscriber is primarily a fashion-savvy professional woman who enjoys charity functions, culture, fine food, and travel.**
- **What is your elevator pitch? This is a one- to three-sentence explanation of what you do for a living that could be told in the amount of time it would take to go up a floor in an elevator.**

Many business networking events, masterminds, meetups, and online groups allow business owners to stand up and present their elevator pitch, which provides a comfortable place to hone it. Take the time to write it down and commit it to memory. And don't be afraid to tweak or change it down the road, you and your business brand should be positively evolving, getting more fabulous as the years go by for your company.

Introvert, Extrovert, or Ambivert?

Imagine walking into a huge, televised awards ceremony. The photographers are snapping pictures. Everyone seems to know each other as they mingle effortlessly on the red carpet. The ladies are checking each other out to see what the others are wearing.

How do you feel in this situation? Do you want to run and hide? Do you cling to your date's arm? Do you saunter in like you own the place and proceed to introduce yourself with a glowing smile? Some people would truly have the urge to turn and walk back out of the room. Some might even act on that impulse.

Let's take stock of how you naturally interact with people. This will directly impact how you show up, lead, and structure your business.

I am an extremely extroverted person. I recharge by being around people. I garner my best ideas by sharing and communicating with others. I adore being on a stage, being in front of a boardroom, or interacting with my students or readers. I love to improvise and switch things up mid-flow. Even when I was writing my last twelve books, most of my best writing has been done in noisy cafes or diners with the energy and sounds of other people buzzing around me.

Others in my family are the exact opposite. They crave silence and alone time. They need routine, structure, and order to function at their highest level. These introverts don't dislike people. They just need to recharge in a different way.

- **Are you an extrovert, introvert, or a combination (an ambivert)? Does it depend on the setting or task that you are completing?**
- **Do you consider yourself to be a highly private person? What leads you to label yourself this way?**
- **Are you comfortable telling the world who you are and what you are all about?**
- **What is your favorite media to present yourself through? Do you love to write blogs on your website, write about your passions in article form, or maybe**

post other people's videos or inspirational quotes in your posts?

These questions are important because extremely private people can struggle with the concept of self-branding. This is the day and age of social media, where "selfies" and posting where you are located are the norms.

One of the positives of self-branding through a computer for an introvert can be that you don't need to look a person in the eye while you hide under the covers in your room, and find like-minded people to network with on your tablet, phone, or laptop. So online networking can be ideal for the introverts who need to self-brand.

In *Quiet: The Power of Introverts in a World That Can't Stop Talking,* **Susan Cain** explained, "The secret to life is to put yourself in the right lighting. For some, it's a Broadway spotlight; for others, a lamp-lit desk. Use your natural powers—of persistence, concentration, and insight—to do work you love and work that matters."[9] The essence of this is to find your way of being, working, and branding.

Some of the greatest bloggers consider themselves to be introverts. While blogging, they can be introspective and muse about their companies and things that they are passionate about. Whereas people like me, who love to do Facebook and Instagram Live broadcasts, tend to be more extroverted because they enjoy the constant feedback, discussion, and being on display.

Determining your recharging style and communication skills are key to determining the way you should brand yourself.

Regardless of your status as an extrovert or introvert, I believe that you can brand yourself as the empowered entrepreneur that you are!

Inspiration
is —
just a
Story
Away

BALL GOWNS TO YOGA PANTS

CHAPTER FIVE

SUCCESS SECRET #6:

Inspiration is Just a Story Away

"Before dreaming about the future or making plans, you need to articulate what you already have going for you— as entrepreneurs do."
— **REID HOFFMAN**, co-founder LinkedIn

"Those who tell the stories rule the world" is a powerful Native American proverb. If you are able to tell a great story, you can sell, captivate, and influence. Almost all of the great leaders and business icons have been able to tell a great story. Very often they are stories from their own lives.

Our business and personal stories can open the doors for the perfect clients and customers to walk in and purchase our products or services. When you are able to tell your stories and captivate people through writing or social media or on a stage, in a boardroom, or one-on-one while networking, you will begin to attract the right clients and customers into your inner circle and business. Through stories, your customers can relate to you and understand your mission, as well as how you can solve their biggest problems.

My tagline my audience knows from my television show, Empowering Women Radio, *Inspiring Lives Magazine*, and my live broadcasts on social media is "Inspiration is just a story away," and it's more than just a catch phrase: it's the truth. Inspiration really is a story away! If you look at all the stories that I've written, in hundreds of articles and 13 books, you'll see that I often focus on others' stories, but I also tell my own.

Let's look at one of my stories from when I was growing up. I often get asked in interviews about my extreme work ethic, and I think it can be traced back to a story about . . . time.

I recall the thudding noise of the time clock as I punched my hours in on my card. No, I wasn't working in a factory. It was quite the opposite.

While I have spent a lifetime helping those who are impoverished around the world, when I was a teenager, my family was living in a beautiful historical mansion called "Wytchwood" in suburban Ohio.

I was afforded a lavish lifestyle with an indoor and outdoor pool and a variety of luxury amenities because my father worked tirelessly as a top kidney specialist doctor. At the same time, my highly educated mother ran the local theater, volunteered to help AIDs patients, and raised my brother and me right. My mother literally managed the household finances like a boss! I recall her saying that "managing a large home was like running a small town."

My mother, whom I call "Moo," was not your typical doctor's wife. Moo was rarely glam and never could justify spending on things like pedicures and manicures. Pretty but low-maintenance, Moo who ran the local theater most often could be found in jeans and galoshes planting and tending to our acres of land. The neighbors actually mistook her for the "house gardener" because she preferred to do it herself. And that suited her just fine.

I was "married to society" at 18 years of age as a debutante at the local cotillion ball because my family repeatedly provided funding and support to the local children's hospital. It wasn't a true marriage but, rather, a time-honored tradition of dressing in a white gown and being presented to society by your father. You would then sign the official society register.

Each debutante was required to throw a party. When we hosted our debutante event, my mom and I veered from the typical white linen affair that was expected. Instead, we hosted a gift-wrapping party that culminated in a trip in a yellow school bus to pick up kids and their moms at a local homeless shelter. Although only one other debutante decided to attend the McDonald's part of the event, Happy Meals and special presents chosen for the children brought priceless smiles.

I grew up with a pretty affluent lifestyle. At 13, I was rocking the spoiled chick personality because quite frankly, I felt entitled.

I was gliding by in life. Getting low grades. Avoiding responsibility.

Then came the day. My father entered our mudroom just after he had found my brother and me slacking on our chores. We were supposed to be working in the garden and yard to earn our allowance. I am pretty sure I was caught napping when I was supposed to be pulling weeds.

I recall hearing hammering. Then a grumpy, gruff voice called us downstairs. And there it was, hanging on the wall in our mudroom . . . the time clock. An old-fashioned relic that we literally had to stamp with the date and exact time we were on the clock to get our allowance from that point forward.

At that moment, I began to learn work ethic. I needed to earn my pay. Nothing was just going to be handed to me in the real world.

Telling stories like this from my past helps people understand where I am coming from. And it provides authentic insights into my personality. When I tell stories, I can connect to people's hearts or simply help them relate to me. People buy from people they know, respect, and trust, especially the higher ticket items you are selling.

With today's social media and traditional media, being able to tell your story is important. Whether you aspire to someday write a book about your expertise or if you just need to communicate your story on Instagram through visuals, storytelling is vital in today's entrepreneur's bag of tricks.

I cannot tell you how many people approach me because they know that I am an author and the editor-in-chief at *Inspiring Lives Magazine*, (everywhere from the grocery store to networking events), and they say, "You know, I've got a story in me."

Today, you can share your content, spread your brand, market your business, and tell people who you are through a variety of platforms. Some of the different ways include a book, a blog post, a magazine article, or a speaking script. Maybe you want to be a TEDx speaker, but you need to master words to be able to do any of these things successfully.

Most of the top entrepreneurs are also storytellers. Let's take **Sara Blakely** for example. She talks about people she wanted as clients ripping up her business card in front of her or simply hanging up on her while she tried to sell fax machines. Her father wanted her to be a lawyer, but she failed the LSAT, more than once. She was disappointed that she wasn't even the right height to be her dream character Goofy when she worked at Disney. But when she cut up her control top pantyhose, Blakely held in her hands what would be the start of a billion-dollar empire.[10]

From the beginning of her enterprise, telling her story, her way, as a mother of four and CEO of Spanx has been important. On stages around the world and in media, she tells stories that are relatable to her customers.

Oprah (another fantastic storyteller who became America's first African-American multibillionaire, based on her inspiring media empire) named Spanx as a favorite product on the Favorite Things Show. The show aired on Nov. 17, 2000, and on the *Oprah* show, Blakely told her story of getting doors slammed in her face as she tried to sell her concept of Spanx. Yet, when she watched Oprah say on television that she too cut up her own pantyhose . . . Blakely exclaimed, "I am not crazy!

Oprah does it too! That was what I needed to then throw my entire heart into what I was doing."

Blakely's stories about her upbringing and creating her empire from scratch are relatable and empowering. She talks about the impact of her father encouraging her to talk about her failures and giving her **Wayne Dyer** motivational audio recordings during a difficult time as a teenager. How she started an empire at 27 with only $5,000 in savings. And how since she didn't have any marketing funds, "I went out on the road and stood in department stores for nine hours a day, lifting up my trouser leg to show customers my tights," Blakely explained to the UK's *Daily Mail* that she went so far as to hold up "pictures of my own bottom, in my white trousers, with and without my product on."

From those humble beginnings, telling her story in malls and using her own bum as the model, she went on to become the first self-made female billionaire on the cover of *Forbes*! And then, in a selfless act of philanthropy, she was the first female to join the Giving Pledge with **Bill and Melinda Gates** and **Warren Buffett** to vow to give away at least half of their riches to charities. Blakely's story is one of a self-made female empire builder with four children and an authentic giving heart.

It's time to start looking at your story. Think through the stories that you have told over the years that people related to, leaned in to hear more, teared up, or chuckled over. Maybe you told them in a classroom, at a cocktail party, or from a stage. Or maybe you haven't told it in public, but you know it should be told. Think about the stories from your life and write out a sentence or two for each of these prompts:

What story can you authentically tell that will help readers, an audience, or clients learn more about:

- . . . a failure or obstacle that you have faced in your life?
- . . . when you conquered a goal that was important to you?
- . . . a childhood memory that molded you into who you are today?
- . . . why you became an entrepreneur?
- . . . a particularly funny or impactful moment in your career?

Many business gurus have a pain point that became their tipping point, which later becomes part of their entrepreneurial identify. For me, it was my unexpected divorce with a three- and five-year-old counting on me to raise them right while I was working crazy hours as a professor; I manifested my dream career to refocus on them. I personally identify myself as a "mompreneur" because I always keep family first while running my business and encourage my Inspiring Lives team to do the same for their families.

Another extremely famous mompreneur is *Jessica Alba*, the co-founder and president of The Honest Company. This Hollywood actress, who started her movie career when she was 13-years-old, struggled to find eco-friendly, safe, and affordable childcare and home products after she became a mom and her family suffered an allergic reaction from laundry detergent. The company hit "unicorn" status, which in the venture capital world means that it hit the elusive, almost mythical, valuation of a billion dollars in their privately held startup company. Alba's The Honest Company grew from her experience, as she explained, "I never expected to run a business, but when I was pregnant with my first daughter, I did what all new moms do—I set out to make a healthy home." She even created a special space at The Honest Company's headquarters where the children of the employees can be entertained and play while their parents are on a mission to "empower people to live healthy, happy lives."[11]

- **How does your family fit into your business plan and your chosen profession?**
- **Can you find ways to incorporate them, automate, or delegate so you can spend less time working and more quality time with your friends and family?**

Gabrielle Bernstein is considered to be a "spirtualpreneur," and as a motivational speaker and #1 *New York Times* bestselling author, she often tells of her journey from substance abuse to healing from addiction and transforming into a "Spirit Junkie." Now she makes meditations and other spiritual work accessible for everyday people through platforms such as Oprah's SuperSoul Sundays and by teaching courses online that show other spiritual entrepreneurs how to create abundant businesses. After all, as Bernstein believes, "The world needs more people bringing love, light and inspiration to their work, no matter what field you're in."[12]

- **Do you have a dark time in your past that you now draw strength from, knowing that you made it to the**

light of the end of the tunnel? If so, what was it, and what was the positive outcome?

- **Your courses, educational tools, books, masterminds, and more can all now be delivered online, making you part of a multibillion-dollar self-education industry. What have you learned to the point of being an expert that you could teach others online?**

Dr. Erin Fall Haskell greeted me with a warm smile, self-awareness, and grace. Incredibly stylish and beautiful, her inner peace shone through when I met her the first time on the set of *Good Morning La La Land.* After we taped the daily live talk show in Hollywood, we had an amazing conversation about being a "soulpreneur" CEO focused on helping other women rise while staying grounded and centered. Dr. Erin says that, "Anyone who is a soulpreneur is working on bringing truth and healing to the world."[13]

Her story of realizing how vital the soul was began when she was pregnant and her baby died in her womb in the ninth month. In an *Inspiring Lives Magazine* interview, Dr. Erin talked about the day after he passed, when she birthed her stillborn son. "The mortician set up a room for me to say goodbye. I was in the dark room alone with his body and I just realized that he was gone. But his body was still here, and I realized we're clearly not the bodies. It made me commit to my personal journey of healing and trying to figure out what the heck we're doing here, and that is what landed me 22 years later to be a Doctor of Divinity."

Now Dr. Erin is on a daily mission in collaboration with her co-hosts **Rob Mack** and *Jezlan* to bring positivity and inspiration to Hollywood and the world through the very first daily live talk show, *Good Morning LaLa Land*. Plus, she holds monthly masterminds called Soulciété, which she envisions someday becoming the number one spiritual leader community in the world. She encourages other to make their careers within the passions that move their souls.

Business leaders have messages that they need to convey, either about themselves, about their personal brand, or about their business. Regardless of whether you're doing an article or a book, focus on what you really want your audience to find out about. You have to know your purpose and make sure that you stay true to what your audience or readers are seeking.

- **In your stories, what do you want to reveal about yourself?**
- **What message do you want to tell about your business in the stories that you tell?**
- **What is your greater purpose as a business owner?**
- **What is your one story that always evokes an emotion or a positive reaction for an audience?**
- **Tell or write that story now, and be sure that it has all the elements of a good story (e.g., plot, characters, conflict, and resolution).**

Remember that if you write a book to support what you are doing with your business it is most likely not going to be your road to easy riches. In fact, some business owners only make enough off of the sale of the book to cover printing and shipping. Why is this? Because with millions of book titles on Amazon.com today, the competition to get books in the hands of readers is fierce. However, if you write a book about what you know, it can become your calling card. It will give you credibility and show clients and investors that you are the expert in your niche and field.

Many people ask me how they can write a book. I believe that blog posts or articles are helpful launching points for finally writing the book that you know could help grow your business. **Cori Wamsley** the former executive editor of *Inspiring Lives Magazine* teaches business owners how to write books to help their companies. Cori stated, "It's always helpful to get some sort of experience in writing first. It will make you feel a lot more comfortable with the writing process itself, and it gives you confidence."

Plus, when you write a book, you begin by creating the chapters in a table of contents. Then from there, it is similar to writing articles for each chapter on the subjects that you outlined. Blogging and article writing not only give great exposure to your company and brand but can also help you hone your writing skills. Find topics that you may be passionate about to someday write a great book about the theme.

- **If your dream is to one day write a book, what would it be about?**
- **Ready to start the process? Write out your Table of Contents for your book.**

Whether you tell your stories in short social media posts or in a whole book, your stories—both personal and professional—can truly affect the clients who are drawn to your business. Make sure that you always include the elements of a good story, know your audience, and determine the right tale to tell for the situation at hand. And remember, "Inspiration is just a story away!"

Entrepreneurs Must Buckle Up for a Roller Coaster Ride of Emotions

BALL GOWNS TO YOGA PANTS

CHAPTER SIX

SUCCESS SECRET #7:

Entrepreneurs Must Buckle Up for a Roller Coaster Ride of Emotions

"When times are bad is when the real entrepreneurs emerge."
— **ROBERT KIYOSAKI**, founder of Cashflow
Technologies Inc. and author of *Rich Dad, Poor Dad*

There will be struggles in your entrepreneurial journey. It's a rollercoaster emotionally and financially. I know because I have been there myself. Many days, I have wondered why I let go of my safety net of a salaried position with benefits and the comfort of a steady paycheck.

Famous technology entrepreneur, investor, and engineer ***Elon Musk*** explained it this way, "Starting a company is like staring into the abyss and eating glass." Some of the most common struggles that entrepreneurs face include:

- **Cash flow and payroll concerns**
- **Wearing all of the hats**
- **Mom or partner guilt**
- **Client issues**
- **Tech support issues**
- **Employee or team challenges**

I have faced all of these issues over the years of running my company. All CEOs and industry leaders have faced these very real challenges. Even authors who have writing empires have faced them.

J.K. Rowling is now a billionaire with over 500 million copies of her books sold from the bestselling book series in history. It all began with *Harry Potter and the Philosopher's Stone*, and this led to (at the time of this publication) six bestselling books and eight blockbuster movie hits. However, over a dozen United Kingdom publishing houses rejected Rowling, and her editor told her she needed a day job because it was, according to him, impossible to make a living writing children's books.

Let's look at the words of Joanne Rowling (who uses "J.K. Rowling" as her penname so her books will appeal to both boys and girls) in her commencement speech at Harvard University in 2008. In her speech about the rollercoaster of setting off to pursue a dream that is not the traditional path, Rowling admitted that she had even contemplated suicide when, "I was jobless, a lone parent, and as poor as it is possible to be in modern Britain, without being homeless." Rowling continued in this epic speech, which I quoted from the transcripts, to say:

> Now, I am not going to stand here and tell you that failure is fun. That period of my life was a dark one, and I had no idea that there was going to be what the press has since represented as a kind of fairy tale resolution. I had no idea then how far the tunnel extended, and for a long time, any light at the end of it was a hope rather than a reality.
>
> So why do I talk about the benefits of failure? Simply because failure meant a stripping away of the inessential. I stopped pretending to myself that I was anything other than what I was, and began to direct all my energy into finishing the only work that mattered to me. Had I really succeeded at anything else, I might never have found the determination to succeed in the one arena I believed I truly belonged. I was set free, because my greatest fear had been realised, and I was still alive, and I still had a daughter whom I adored, and I had an old typewriter and a big idea. And so rock bottom became the solid foundation on which I rebuilt my life.[14]

Many entrepreneurs have experienced dramatic highs and lows in their lives. The most amazing stories I have heard in my years of interviewing, mentoring, and teaching thousands of incredible leaders are about how they use their pain to help others. Many have ended up forming or partnering with charities that align with their visions.

Giving back through charitable works and funding is an important part of many entrepreneurs' plans. As the president and founder of the Global Sisterhood 501 (c)(3) public charitable organization www.GlobalSisterhoodOnline. org, I adore giving back to help women and children around the world. I chose my publisher for this book (Morgan James) based on their charitable partnerships with Operation Underground Railroad, The National Center for the Prevention of Community Violence, and Habitat for Humanity. Since 2006, Morgan James founder, **David Hancock** explained, "We place the Habitat [for Humanity] logo on the back and inside of our books, with a statement of our passion for the organization and raising awareness for the organization's life-changing work, helping low-income families build decent homes they can afford to buy."[15] Heart-aligned business owners who create their own wealth often find charities to pour back into.

Tony Robbins, the number 1 bestselling author, philanthropist, and expert life and business strategist, grew up in poverty. He was so desperate for knowledge at one point that he had to save his money from being a janitor in high school to be able to attend his first seminar and learn from his mentor **Jim Rohn**. Now, Robbins teaches in football stadiums and coaches presidents, billionaire celebrities, and royalty. He has empowered more than 50 million people from 100 countries through his audio and video life training programs.

Yet, even though he is now wildly financially successful, Robbins explained in a press release, "I'll never forget what it felt like as a young boy thinking we wouldn't be able to sit down to Thanksgiving dinner. Then a stranger gave us the food we couldn't afford. It's heartbreaking that in the wealthiest country in the world, 40 million Americans, including more than 12 million children, may not know where their next meal is coming from. I'll never stop working to eradicate hunger in America."[16]

Robbins helps feed 100 million people a year through Feeding America˙, the largest hunger-relief organization in the United States. After starting its partnership with him, Feeding America recently announced that it is changing the name of its "100 Million Meals Challenge" to the "1 Billion Meals Challenge" to reflect the campaign's new goal of helping provide 1 billion meals by 2025! Launched in 2014, the campaign has already raised funds to help provide more than 420 million meals to hungry Americans through the Feeding America network of 200 member food banks and 60,000 food pantries and meal programs. This is thanks in part to Robbins' matching gifts, which have included both personal donations and all proceeds from his two most-recent books: *Money: Master the Game* and *Unshakeable*. For every dollar raised, Feeding America helps provide at least 10 meals through its network of food banks.

- **What charitable element of volunteering time, energy, talent, or funds could your company pour into?**
- **Will you partner with registered charitable organizations? If so, which ones align with your company's mission?**

- **Will you form your own nonprofit? If so, you must follow a completely different set of procedures, but it can be a tremendous blessing to be able to serve the needs of others. If you commit to running a charity, I suggest procuring legal advice from a lawyer and building a strong executive board to help you navigate nonprofit creation and sustainability.**

So if you have that big idea, if you claim that dream as your own, if you are ready to live it during the waking hours, you need to commit to your idea and begin your Empowered Entrepreneur Action Plan!

Being

the Best

in a Noisy Market Means

Digging Deep,

Working Hard,

& Providing a

Stellar Product

or Service

BALL GOWNS TO YOGA PANTS

CHAPTER SEVEN:

SUCCESS SECRET #8:

Being the Best in a Noisy Market Means Digging Deep, Working Hard, and Providing a Stellar Product or Service

"Be undeniably good. No marketing effort or social media buzzword can be a substitute for that."
— **ANTHONY VOLODKIN**, founder of Hype Machine

You *can* be the best in your niche area. You just have to dig deep, do your research, work hard, and provide a stellar product or service. Because so many industries like marketing or online coaching are saturated and are readily available around the world at the click of a button, you need to determine what sets you apart from the crowd. You need to do it differently and often better than your competition.

- **What will make you and your company stand out?**
- **What will be the main strengths of your company?**

Beyond your strengths, it can be very helpful to examine what other successful companies think of as their "truths." The billionaire founders of Google, **Larry Page** and **Sergey Brin** began their venture when they were doctoral students at Stanford University.

Google's mission as a corporation is "to organize the world›s information and make it universally accessible and useful."[17] We all have different missions for our companies, and earlier in this book, you began to flesh out what your mission is for your business.

Now, let's examine Google's "Ten Things We Know to be True" that Page and Brin first wrote just a few years into starting their company.[18] **Jonathan Moules** in *The Rebel Entrepreneur: Rewriting the Business Rulebook* stated, "We are all dot.coms now, thank goodness."[19] Let's look at a dot.com that has truly flourished through the lens of a successful entrepreneur.

Google Truth #1. Focus on the user, and all else will follow.

Google focuses on the computer user's experience and strives to serve their needs first and foremost. For example, they provide clear and simple fast-loading pages because that is needed when searching online.

As an entrepreneur, you need to look at what your clients and customers really need. This is vital whether you are running a business, writing a book, or running a nonprofit. Knowing who you are doing it for and what is important to them is key. Plus, being sure that you can provide what they need is important as well. Build on that knowledge with a superior product or service.

- **Who are your potential clients? Describe their demographics (e.g., age range).**
- **What does the person who purchases what your company will provide need?**
- **What is your plan to survey or ask your clients what they need so you can focus on the user's needs?**

Google Truth #2. It's best to do one thing really, really well.

As Google simply explained, "We do search." And they continued on to say that they "solve complex issues and provide continuous improvements to a service that already makes finding information a fast and seamless experience for millions of people."

Google does "search" very well. Google has multiple products from Google Maps to Google Scholar, yet they all boil down to the element of "searching."

My company Inspiring Lives International does "inspiring" really well. Maybe you do "baking" very well, so you will be a baker who sells your cookies and cupcakes out of a store front and online. If you are great at "coaching" others, get specific, and decide to be the best business coach for women. Or if your YouTube tutorials on how to apply makeup are getting millions of hits because you custom-blend your makeup, maybe a makeup product line is in your future.

Determine the one thing that you truly do exceptionally well, and then strive to build a company that has that at the heart of the business.

- **In one word, what will your company do really, really well?**
- **What products or services will you provide that are proof that you do that one thing very well?**
- **Are there other products or services that you could add to your company in the future that could add more income streams while still focusing on what your customers need and that one thing that you will do really, really well?**

Google Truth #3. Fast is better than slow.

In our fast-paced digital world, people are used to instant gratification. Time is valuable, and efficiency is important. From their Google Chrome browser to their website's loading time, Google knows that time is of the essence. Think about how you feel waiting in a long line, forever for your meal, or for a website to load. Your experience affects how you view that company.

I went through the wringer with the university textbook I authored that was heavily internally reviewed. Over twenty experts gave their opinion on each chapter, and it took three years to complete because it was a rigorous scholarly process. By the time the book was being used in universities, I was confident that it would be well-received by the university students around the world, though. I love to read my Amazon reviews, usually because I like to hear what my readers learned through my writing. I deeply value these reviews and am usually so grateful for them!

However, when my textbook for future teachers came out and I checked my reviews, my heart dropped when I saw only two out of five stars! I was crushed and wondered what I did wrong as the author. Then I read the comment. It said that they gave it two stars because the delivery of the book was slow, not that my writing was poor.

In today's market, slow can equal bad reviews no matter the product. Negative reviews on sites such as Amazon or Yelp can potentially be devastating for a small business. You need to work to keep it all moving at a quick pace for your customers.

- **What will be your policy on speed? For example, will you try to do quick deliveries, 24-hour turn around on emailed questions, or fast webpage loading?**
- **How could you make your company function faster without sacrificing quality?**

Google Truth #4. Democracy on the web works.

"Google search works because it relies on the millions of individuals posting links on websites to help determine which other sites offer content of value." And Google uses their patented PageRank™ algorithm, which analyzes which sites have been "voted" to be the best sources of information by other pages across the web. Within a democracy, the people have the power through a system of representation. People determine Google's rankings.

People will decide how you are perceived online and offline as well, and they will want a way to voice their opinions. When I worked at the university, we had what the president called "Town Hall Meetings" where students could express what they needed from their school. My gym collected comment cards for years and then did a total top-to-bottom upgrade and remodel to meet the needs of the athletic club members. We survey our *Inspiring Live Magazine* readers through social media to determine what they are seeking in our magazine. Giving a voice to your clients will have them coming back for more once they see that their ideas and opinions matter.

- **How could you give the people you will serve with your company a say in what you are providing?**
- **What questions could you ask in a survey to determine how you could continuously provide what the people need from your company?**
- **What is one complaint or change you think your customers would state if you asked for their opinion in the future? How will you make that change?**

Google Truth #5. You don't need to be at your desk to need an answer.

In our mobile modern world, "People want access to information wherever they are, whenever they need it." Google went on to explain that they offer "new solutions for mobile services that help people all over the globe to do any number of tasks on their phone, from checking email and calendar events to watching videos, not to mention the several different ways to access Google search on a phone."

Making your website, shopping, and support all available on mobile platforms from Android to iPads is important.

We made sure that when *Inspiring Lives Magazine* went through a website update that the layout was as great from a phone as a desktop. Also, when we started the *Inspiring Lives Magazine* app, at first it was not very functional, so we went back to the drawing board to see how we could make it more compelling for readers. We also found ways to make the app a revenue generator by providing a digital magazine issue for a smaller fee than the print version. With the *Inspiring Lives Magazine* app, you as a reader can have "Inspiration in the palm of your hand."

- **If you have a website already, grab your phone, and do a spot check of your company's mobile platform (if you don't yet, keep these elements in mind as you create one):**
  - o **Does your website still look aesthetically pleasing and on brand across platforms?**
  - o **Do the pages load well?**
  - o **What could be changed to best represent your business through technology?**
- **If you created an app in the future, what would its function and purpose be?**

When it came time to expand our sales impact with technology, the company continuously was led back to the online funnel method of delivery for our motivational media products and services.

A fellow Morgan James published author, **Russell Brunson**, author of the *New York Times* bestselling book *Dot.Com Secrets*, co-founded ClickFunnels® based on a need to create income without constantly selling from the stage since it was taking time away from his wife Collette and their five children.[20]

Brunson started selling online in college, peddling everything from shakes and supplements to t-shirts and technology services. His company quickly grew to be worth $100,000,000, and by 2018, his teaching, training, and software had helped create over 200 millionaires in an exclusive group they call the "2 Comma Club." Brunson is deeply committed to giving back as he gives a portion of sales to World Teacher Aide to help schools in Africa and is dedicated to helping Operation Underground Railroad rescue children from sex trafficking internationally. As Brunson has said, "We all have a mission. We have something we can do to change someone's life."

We utilized the ClickFunnels system for marketing the message of Inspiring Lives to get it out into the world. It helps us create a quick system of delivery for webinars and direct sales so we have satisfied customers. They don't have to search for what they need because the funnel directs them right to it, and I can explain to the customer through video and sales pages what we offer so they can purchase right away.

- **What technology could you use on the back end of your business to help you sell your products or services? For example, if you have online courses, you**

> may need an education platform such as Teachable˚
> or Kajabi˚.
> - If you had used a funnel-type of automated marketing
>   tool, what would you set it up to do? For example,
>   I created a leads funnel for my EmpowerU Master
>   Class so the right women around the world could
>   work with me to find inspiration, empowerment,
>   balance, and abundance in their businesses and lives.

Google Truth #6. You can make money without doing evil.

Google is a business that generates revenue through advertising and offering search technology for companies. They serve all their users by adhering to a set of guiding principles for advertising: ads are relevant to the pages, they aren't flashy pop-ups, and advertising is clearly identified as a "Sponsored Link."

> - What policies and guidelines will you adhere to
>   in your company to be known as trustworthy and
>   ethical?
> - What should you add to your company-wide policies
>   that would assure that you and your employees are
>   functioning with high integrity?

Google Truth #7. There's always more information out there.

After they made websites searchable, Google went on to get more creative with accessibility of information, " . . . like adding the ability to search news archives, patents, academic journals, billions of images, and millions of books. And our researchers continue looking into ways to bring all the world's information to people seeking answers."

There is always room for improvement and growth in a company. When Google leveled up, they had to think outside of the box of traditional website searching and take their business to new heights.

- **If you were to "level up" your company in the future, what would the changes be to your product, service, office space, and more?**
- **What would you need to go to the next level with your company in a few years (e.g., more marketing and PR, a new employee, funding, new construction)?**

Google #8. The need for information crosses all borders.

Google strives to provide the whole world with information in every language. They have offices in more than 60 countries. Using Google translation tools, I have had meaningful discussions and even conducted business with people who speak languages that I don't speak. Google understands the need for a global community and everyone's need for information.

When I was a professor in the Instructional Management and Leadership Ph.D. program at Robert Morris University, some of my colleagues thought I was nuts to use Facebook as my platform for connecting my students with people from my network. At the time, some in academia frowned upon the idea of being connected on social media with students.

Many thought it dissolved the boundaries needed for a typical professor/student relationship. However, it proved to be the perfect way for genuine connections to happen while I taught the Global Perspective course. The future leaders of schools, businesses, and nonprofits were matched up with mentors around the world while they were crafting their own Global Action Plans for their futures.

As the president of the Global Sisterhood 501(c)(3) public charity, I have utilized brilliant friendships around the world beyond borders. It all began when I was contacted by a woman in rural Pakistan who had heard an interview I conducted on Empowering Women Radio. The show she heard featured **Haseena Patel** in South Africa. For years, I have been Skyping into the classrooms in Haseena's high school academy to help guide Empowerment Circles, teaching vision boarding and building self-esteem.

"Do you know what you are doing here?" the woman in Pakistan asked me. Her predecessor at the empowerment organization she ran had been shot and killed outside their building for her women's rights work. After she convinced me that I was the journalist to tell her important story to the world, she showed me the power of the internet for removing boundaries. I simply shrugged when she asked me the question about what I was doing on our video chat.

She explained that by connecting so many empowered women through their life stories and through authentic friendship, I was creating a "true Global Sisterhood." Following the conversation that named us, the seeds of a charity were planted. Now the Global Sisterhood has a thriving

#PopUpGiving program to help women and children who come to us with needs, and women contribute internationally to make it happen. From supporting the championship winning Super Ladies soccer team in Ghana to helping build a beautiful brick school in Pakistan where they used to learn in the hot sun under tented sheets with holes in them, The Global Sisterhood truly is a change agent thanks to tearing down borders and building up sisterhood.

Whether it is a nonprofit organization or a for-profit business you are running, think about how you could expand your company and ideas internationally. It could help expand your network while boosting your giving or profit.

- **How could you include a global perspective in your business?**
- **What would you need to consider if you go global with your company? For example, when we do business internationally, we have to consider the shipping costs or customs issues.**
- **How could you make your website and marketing materials more customer-friendly for people around the world? For example, have multiple races and exceptionalities represented in your visuals in your social media, marketing brochures, and website.**

Google #9. You can be serious without a suit.

"Our atmosphere may be casual, but as new ideas emerge in a café line, at a team meeting or at the gym, they are traded, tested and put into practice with dizzying speed—and they may be the launch pad for a new project destined for worldwide use." Google gets this.

As does Inspiring Lives International, my company! During the summer, all the mompreneurs in our company love to have team meetings poolside in bathing suits. We work from our phones and iPads while our kiddos play in the water. We have spa days together and even slumber parties. My team is often found together at red carpet events, at award shows, and at fundraisers for charities that we support, together.

These unique settings (that sometimes include boardrooms but more often means an unusual setting), builds on our unique Inspiring Lives team culture. We embrace the idea that you don't need to wear a suit to get work done. We have taken our business to the next level in gowns, PJs, or even a bikini. As a boss, I believe that a long hike in the woods in the fresh air talking with my vice president can be the perfect office setting for the real inspiring brainstorming to occur!

Today's entrepreneur doesn't have to be confined by the traditional office space or power suit. Think about your ideal work environment and style.

- **Describe your ideal working vibe and setting.**
- **What would you wear to work daily or on occasion if you could wear whatever you want?**
- **Where and how could you make your ideal work environment a reality?**

Google #10. "Great" just isn't good enough.

Between Christmas Eve dinner and dessert, I was busily washing dishes in my kitchen when my young son in his hooded dragon PJs walked up to me and handed me a white envelope. On the front, he had scrawled in pen with his elementary school spelling "RESUMAE." He told me that he was the boss, and I had a job interview in his office in a few minutes. Jacob told me that I needed to be prepared.

I was very curious about what in the world he was talking about. Multiple generations were talking up a storm in the dining room as they waited for me to get desert out to them, but they would have to wait.

I left the dishes in the sink and sneaked over to my home office. There, perched on my brown leather desk chair behind my huge mahogany desk was my son. He was wearing his PJs, with a very serious look on his face. Jacob instructed me to take a seat because he had questions. He explained that he owned two companies and needed to see which I would be best suited to work for.

He explained that his first company was a video game company and that they were doing quite well. He grabbed a sheet of paper and quickly drew a zig-zag line with an arrow pointing up at the end. He said, "This is our profits, now. But, what could you do to keep them going up?" I was pleasantly shocked by this, but of course, I went into full-on acting mom mode.

I first asked him what my job would be. He said, "Well, you would just be typing all day." I explained to him that a job like that would be a waste of my skills. He sat up a bit when I explained that I was a good idea person, I lead people well. If we use my teaching talents, we could move from good to amazing. My son's dimples appeared as a smile spread across his face. He drew another diagonal line straight up on another sheet of paper. He held the two line drawings side-by-side and said, "I see us growing even more with you teaching my team!"

I asked if I got the job (knowing that I had to get back to my Christmas Eve guests in the other room). He didn't answer me. Instead, he said he needed to show me his other company. He hurriedly glanced around the room, grabbed the blue Styrofoam packaging from inside a modem box under my desk, and examined it.

Jacob thought for a minute and exclaimed, "My other company makes couches!" He held it at angle so I could see that the front was cut like a mini couch. His vocabulary wowed me when he said, "This is a prototype. But you can see the front is a couch. Right behind it, there is a built-in place for the dogs and the kids to play." He pointed to a shallow hole in the packing material that would indeed be the perfect playpen for the kids or pets! I exclaimed that it was a very cool idea, and it would be highly marketable for families so they could be together in the living room and yet all have their own space.

Before he shook my hand and told me that I had the job, my new pretend boss told me that he wanted both of his businesses to be amazing. He wanted to hire me for both of his companies! This of course made this imagination-loving mom's heart smile.

When we got back for dessert, I briefly explained our roleplaying game to my mother. She said "It sounds like somebody is watching you run your company. And maybe even listening to your EmpowerU Master Class videos!"

I love that my children are learning to grow their ideas into a possible business. Yet, even if they never run companies, the idea of constantly striving for the best in all areas of life will serve them well.

As Google explained in their "Ten Things We Know to be True" statement, "We see being great at something as a starting point, not an endpoint . . . We're always looking for new places where we can make a difference. Ultimately, our constant dissatisfaction with the way things are becomes the driving force behind everything we do."

- **What would it look like and feel like to have your company be the best version of your business vision?**
- **When you think about your company in the future, what would make you feel dissatisfied?**
- **Write down what would bring you satisfaction. Be very specific in what you would need to earn to feel like a success with your company.**

Look at what others have done to be successful with their businesses. Then see how you can do your own version and truly shine in your niche market. Whether you are learning from a mentor, reading books, getting coached, attending conferences, or even watching YouTube videos, keep learning and thinking beyond the basics. Basic is boring and won't get you matched with customers in a saturated market. You may want to create a list of YOUR company's truths as you strive to be the best at what your company offers!

Armed with Your
Dream Team
You Can
Make
It —
Happen

CHAPTER EIGHT:

SUCCESS SECRET #9:

Armed with Your Dream Team, You Can Make It Happen

"Change creates unprecedented opportunity. But to take full advantage of those opportunities, focus on the team. Teams win."

— JOHN DOERR

It was one of the greatest team-building experiences I have ever had in my life, and I was 40 feet in the air in the trees. The year was 2001, and here is an excerpt from what I wrote in my first doctoral journal, (complete with quotes from the leadership books I was reading at the time) about the amazing experience of becoming part of a team…

"No voice ever sounded as sweet as the ones that cheered me on as I tried to conquer the 'Cyclops' obstacles. It was during my adventure at the Linsly Outdoor Center as I began my journey to my doctorate. As I stood on the ground staring up a tall, looming tree complete with ropes, tires, and pegs for foot holds, a wave of insecurity rushed through my being. My fellow cohort members encouraged me from the moment I stepped near the tree. They wanted me to go first. With fear in the pit of my stomach but determination in my soul and on my face, I began to climb. I shimmied my way up using brute strength, agility, and strategy for where to place my hands and feet.

"Sooner than I would have imagined, I was amazingly close to the top. I could hear the voices rising from the base of the tree. Someone said, 'Wow! She almost has it.' Then someone yelled, 'If anyone can do it, *you* can do it, Shellie,' and 'You are almost there!' I heard them, and although it registered with my mind, my soul had not heard it yet. My arms were tired and bruised, my muscles were exhausted, and my ego said I simply couldn't get up that last step.

"The rope I had to grab dangled above me as a physical representation of my insecurities. I could see the tire that I so desperately wanted to swing my legs into. With every try, I got closer and closer. But the rope was so thin, and the tire seemed so far away. Soon I realized that the possibility of falling was so great and, in my mind, inevitable. So, I wrapped the rope around my arms from the inside. When I did almost fall, I was glad that I could pick myself up again. My arms were rubbed raw from the rope, but I knew I had to remain close to my goal to be able to reach it.

"Time and time again, I tried. Then I asked my new friend Bruce to stand where I could see him. Bruce and I had already formed a bond through our teamwork. According to *Soar with your Strengths* by **Donald O. Clifton** and **Paula Nelson**, 'A relationship is the process of investing in another person by doing something for that person's own good without consideration of self-reward.'[21]

"Bruce called up to me, 'Shellie, do you want me to sing your song?' As he began to sing 'Amazing Grace,' I knew that this special member of my cohort understood that I needed that extra push of external motivation. The night before, I had sung 'Amazing Grace' to express through my favorite medium the incredible internal transformation that we were all experiencing.

"As **Lee G. Bolman** and **Terrence E. Deal** put it in *Leading with Soul*, 'When each of us plunges into the depths of the core of our being, there we find soul.' As he sang, I remembered that I do have gifts to be shared and my goals can and will be reached. For the first time I could actually see myself being able to accomplish this task.[22]

"**Clifton** and **Nelson** explain that, 'Visualization is the process by which we mentally rehearse.' I then swung my legs up through the tire, lifted myself onto the goal, and proudly stood up. I announced to the forest and my team that WE did it!"

When you have a team of people who fill in each other's skill gaps, you can accomplish every goal. Armed with your dream team, you can make your business happen. However, even taking that step toward hiring your first employee or trusting a partner can seem daunting for the solopreneur just beginning to build a business.

Let's start with the first person that you bring on your team. Maybe it will be a virtual assistant or a person who will help you develop and organize the actual business. The most important hire I ever made was **Kelly Frost**, who is now my CMO. Because I am a creative/big picture-thinker, I have always struggled with the budgeting and number crunching that is vital for a business, especially when the business is growing in leaps and bounds as we are now. Kelly's background was in HR, accounting, and media. This made her the perfect fit and a main reason that I was able to grow my company with a solid foundation.

Another great hire was **Cori Wamsley** who has been a friend for years. My own mother had been proofreading and editing my hundreds of articles and half of my books, and there came a point when she admitted that it was time for her to do her own writing. I went to Cori for her amazing word-crafting support years ago and never looked back. I know that my words are in good hands with Cori as I create my books and articles, and she even served as the executive editor of my *Inspiring Lives Magazine*.

When it comes to my team at *Inspiring Lives Magazine*, we quickly realized that a strong sales team would be required to procure advertisements for the magazine and sponsorships for events such as the Empowering Women Awards. We have assembled a fantastic team that supports each other in their sales and networks together for the benefit of our entire group. Plus, they work in conjunction with our creative director and social media coordinator as they craft fantastic magazine layouts, media posts, and advertisements for our clients that sell their products and services to our readers. Teamwork and work flow has been especially important in this arm of our company.

I gave you a peek into the inner working of my *Inspiring Lives Magazine* team. Now, we need to think about what team members you need to create your dream staff. Let's think through your team:

- **Who comprises your team right now, and what are their responsibilities?**
- **What gaps do you have in your own skill set? What tasks do you have daily that you would benefit from having someone take over?**
- **List 3 interview questions that you will ask before checking references and hiring people on to your company.**

  a.

  b.

  c.

- **What will your hiring and onboarding look like? Who will conduct these activities?**
- **What type of training will you provide for your new employees so they can get up to speed on your company and their craft?**

Before you hire someone for your company, be sure that they are a good fit for the culture that you have created with your team. The new employee or independent contractor should be ready to dive seamlessly into the job after the contracts are signed and they are trained.

Be sure to check in with your employees regularly, especially if they work remotely. In many businesses today, we don't meet around a water cooler in a break room at the office. So be sure that everyone is clear on their own workflow and feels supported by you as the CEO.

I learned throughout the years of running a company that you must have clear job descriptions for your staff. The job descriptions must be adhered to, yet you should allow for tweaking. Also, when I first started as a boss, I tried to fit employees into jobs that I needed filled without regard to what they particularly excelled at. After leading for years, I realized how much better the tasks were when they could apply their true talent and passion. Getting to know your staff and their abilities and talents is important, and often you can add tasks to their job responsibilities that they are fantastic at, which will bolster their love for their job, increase retention, and strengthen your company.

The benefits of having a team that supports each other and works together well cannot be overestimated. An empowered team will help you focus on your own zone of brilliance and bring structure and flow to the company.

Once you have your team set and you are working hard toward common goals, be sure to motivate the team in ways that will boost their passion for what you are doing together.

My core team is all ladies who happen to all love travel, food, and beauty treatments. We recently did a spa day, delicious dinner, and an overnight at a hotel together to reward the staff for an amazing job going national with *Inspiring Lives Magazine*. Think of creative ways you can reward your staff for a job well done.

- **How can you show your staff that you appreciate them?**

- **What milestones should you celebrate for your business?**

Creating the ideal team for your company can be tricky. You may end up hiring people and then realizing that they are not a good fit. Yet, when you have the right team, or partner, you can work together to create your own dream company. Together, your team can make magic happen as your services and products successfully get out into the world, while you generate a positive revenue stream.

Once You Reach

The Top;

Stay There:
Healthy, Sane, Joyful, &

Serving Your

Greater Purpose

While

Monetizing

Your Business!

BALL GOWNS TO YOGA PANTS

SUCCESS SECRET #10:

Once You Reach the Top, Stay There: Healthy, Sane, Joyful, and Serving Your Greater Purpose While Monetizing Your Business!

"Success is not the key to happiness. Happiness is the key to success. If you love what you are doing, you will be successful."
— **ALBERT SCHWEITZER**, Nobel Prize Laureate

The final chapter of *Ball Gowns to Yoga Pants: Entrepreneurial Secrets for Creating your Dream Business and Brand* marks a tremendous milestone for you! Congratulations on working through the probing questions as you set off to engage in your own entrepreneurial journey. In conclusion, you need a plan, and your business will thrive as you work the plan.

Now is the time to whip out your computer and organize that plan so you and others can refer to it. You may want to refresh your memory by looking back at what you wrote in the pages of this book, as well. *Ball Gowns to Yoga pants: Entrepreneurial Secrets for Creating your Dream Business and Brand* book is the GPS, but you are in the driver's seat.

When I originally set out on my entrepreneurial journey, I thought a long traditional "business plan" was vital. Now that I have been a CEO for years, I see that some things need to be down on paper, and yes, the traditional version is important for gaining capital and funding as well as referring back to be sure that you are on track.

There are many great resources for creating a business plan, including those provided by the Small Business Association and books like **Gino Wickman's** *Traction: Get a Grip on Your Business*. Yet, below, I list the questions that I found from my perspective as a CEO to be imperative for creating a strong, actionable plan beyond establishing your annual revenue goals (which is, of course, very important to creating a profitable company).

Like the rest of this book, take the time to really think through these questions and fill them out. You will find that they are the basis for a successful business plan.

- **Describe your business. Make it clear what your niche is and how you see the future of your company. (Think of this as what your "About Us" page on your**

**website will say about your company, and include
the goals and purpose of your business.)**
- **What are your company's core values?**

By knowing your company's top core values, you will be
able to attract the right team members into your company, hold
your team accountable to standards, and have a solid foundation
for your brand.

Inspiring Lives International has the following Core Values:

1. Support others, and do the right thing.
2. Always be prepared with a solution, not just a problem.
3. Be honest and have integrity.
4. Have a high work ethic and always produce quality.
5. Be the best version of yourself.

The top five core values of your company will be:
1.

2.

3.

4.

5.

- **What products and services do you offer? And what will be the price points for the products and services that you will offer?**
- **What is the competition in your market, and how will you compare and differentiate what you offer? Please take some time to research online because this will prepare you to be able to set yourself apart from the competition.**
- **How will you market and promote your services? Think about traditional media (such as print, television, radio, and billboards), social media, and word of mouth.**
- **What is the ideal future of your company?**

You need to know who will be buying your products and services. I explored this and realized that the target market for my companies' products and services is generally "women entrepreneurs who are seeking inspiration, empowerment, balance, and abundance. They need their tribe of women friends. They are open to change to gain their dream life, and they are honest and vulnerable. They like fashion and travel.

Plus, they have their own compelling personal story and big dreams."

- **What is Your Company's Target Market?**

Company Customer Avatar

When you have created a clear avatar, whether you use a template with questions found online or you craft a story about your ideal customer's persona, you will best be able to market to them because you will use the right language in your copy, frequently post in the social media that they utilize, deliver better products and services, and have targeted advertising.

Here is an example of an imaginary ideal customer story that was created for Inspiring Lives International that tells the likes and needs as a customer and helped my board and team see who our ideal customer would be. Of course, everyone is unique, but knowing who your target client is will help you tailor everything from your products and services to your marketing plan. Karen is the avatar that we created.

"Karen Schienfield has her master's degree and is running a small business as a side hustle. Her day job is in insurance sales in downtown Pittsburgh, and she balances that with her volunteer activities. She is dedicated to keeping #FamilyFirst with her second-husband and two beautiful elementary school-aged kids Mark and Susie. Karen tries to fit in a yoga workout or Zumba classes as often as possible. She loves to get the free skin care gift with purchase at the Clinique counter at the mall or when her best friend says "I love you" before she hangs up the phone. She reads *Marie Claire Magazine*, loves Oprah's

SuperSoul Sunday shows on TV, and reads books like Rachel Hollis' *Girl, Wash Your Face.* Karen loves to meditate listening to Gabrielle Bernstein, the author of *The Universe Has Your Back.* Karen enjoys attending conferences such as body-mind-spirit types of women's retreats. If her face is in her phone, she may be reading blogs such as Scary Mommy or scrolling Instagram and Facebook.

"Her pain points are in the areas of life balance. She is baffled by how her friends' social media feeds always show the perfect work/life balance and loves the aesthetic of the polished life. However, she looks around her and sees that is not necessarily her reality. She is seeking a tribe of like-minded inspiring, ambitious women and wants to learn how to fully step into her definition of success and live her best life. Her objections to the purchase process are that she feels she can piece together the information by herself, make the right contacts, and learn 'all the things' through the internet, so why pay for the retreats, books/magazine, EmpowerU Master Class, and more through Inspiring Lives International?

"Then 37-year-old Karen sighs and looks around her house. She realizes she needs to get dinner prepared (chicken nuggets again for the little ones). Her kiddos are being alarmingly quiet in the other room (which could be trouble). She hasn't had a second to breathe (not that she really could, wearing the tight Spanx under her clothes for her day job that covers her with her health insurance) . . . never-mind sitting down to finally write out that business plan to have her side hustle become a lucrative full time job with flexibility.

"Karen's favorite quote is by Maya Angelou, 'I learned that making a living is not the same as making a life.'"

• **Write your Ideal Customer Avatar for your company.**

Being armed with a solid business plan and a customer avatar are great steps toward crafting your business and brand.

Yet, to have a true sustainable solution as an entrepreneur, you need to also have a plan for your own life: budgeting, networking, family time, and self-care. Stay healthy, sane, and joyful, while serving your greater purpose and monetizing your business. This is so important to true empowerment and avoiding burn out. Take the time to set goals in those areas, and hold yourself to them to ensure a positive solution for you through this experience.

• **How will you take care of yourself well while you build your company?**
• **Where and how will you get leads and new customers?**

As you reach your goals, even the small ones, take the time to celebrate. Remember also that others are on their own entrepreneurial paths, so don't compare your chapter 4 to someone else's chapter 13. We are all at different points in our walk, and you are wasting time if you get stuck in comparison mode with your competition.

Keep learning and growing, constantly seek out new resources, and network for your company's success.

I am proud of your work thus far, and I can't wait to hear from you about your company as you utilize your knowledge from ***Ball Gowns to Yoga Pants: Entrepreneurial Secrets for Creating your Dream Business and Brand***! The secret is out and it's time for you to bring the company you have on your heart to creation and to thrive. You are the CEO of your company and your life. Create your authentic brand and lead your successful business!

ABOUT THE AUTHOR

Dr. Shellie Hipsky is the CEO of Inspiring Lives International, an "Inc. Verified" motivational media company. *The American Chronicle* called her "A top entrepreneur in the U.S.," and *The Huffington Post* categorizes her as a "Fierce Woman." She is the president of the nonprofit 501 (c)(3) the Global Sisterhood, a charity that guides and supports women and girls toward their dreams and goals. Dr. Shellie has earned the titles of "Entrepreneur of the Year in Inspiration and Empowerment," the "Women of Achievement Award," "Best Woman in Business," and "VIP Woman of the Year." Three of her 13 published books, based on 100 amazing interviews from her *Empowering Women Radio* show, the *Common Threads* trilogy focused on *Inspiration, Empowerment,* and *Balance,* earned international bestseller status.

The former tenured professor of Ph.D. students and host of *Inspiring Lives with Dr. Shellie* on NBC has keynoted internationally from Passion to Profits in Hollywood to The University of Oxford in England and now teaches her signature EmpowerU Master Class, making the world her classroom. This powerful entrepreneur and influencer is the founder and editor-in-chief of *Inspiring Lives Magazine: THE Magazine for Empowering Women*, which is available on the app, digital subscription, or at Barnes and Noble nationwide with millions of impressions. She has been featured on over 20 magazine covers and on all the major TV networks.

Dr. Shellie is delighted to bring the world *Ball Gowns to Yoga Pants: Entrepreneurial Secrets to Create Your Dream Business and Brand* through Morgan James Publishing. Dr. Shellie looks forward to hearing how your dream company is created through what you learned in this book through a positive Amazon review. If you want to book her for a keynote or take her EmpowerU Master Class, she can be reached at s.hipsky@inspiringlivesmagazine.com.

ENDNOTES

Ch. 2

1   Frankel, Bethenny. "Bethenny Frankel Says You Need a Personal Mission Statement." Glamour. https://www.glamour.com/story/bethenny-frankel-says-you-need-a-personal-mission-statement (October 20, 2019).

2   Gaines, Johanna. "About Magnolia." Magnolia. https://magnolia.com/about/ (October 20, 2019).

3   Hollis, Rachel. "The Hollis Company." The Chic Site. https://thechicsite.com/2018/05/31/the-hollis-company/ (October 20, 2019).

4   Kane, Libby. "Mrs. Fields Cookies: How Debbi Fields Built an Empire from Scratch." The Muse. https://www.themuse.com/advice/mrs-fields-cookies-how-debbi-fields-built-an-empire-from-scratch (October 13, 2019).

5   Vinton, Kate. "How Two Dermatologists Built A Billion Dollar Brand in Their Spare Time." Forbes.com. https://www.forbes.com/sites/katevinton/2016/06/01/billion-dollar-brand-proactiv-rodan-fields/#72b519e63bfe (October 20, 2019).

6   Hicks, Angie. "About Angie." Angie Hicks. http://www.angiehicks.com/content/about-angie (October 20, 2019).

Ch. 3

7   Gladwell, Malcolm. *The Tipping Point.* New York, NY: Little, Brown & Company, 2000.

8   Kiyosaki, Robert. *Rich Dad, Poor Dad. What the Rich Teach their Kids About Money that the Poor Do Not.* New York, NY: Warner Books, 2017.

Ch. 4

9   Cain, Susan. *Quiet: The Power of Introverts in a World That Can't Stop Talking.* New York, NY: Broadway Paperbacks, 2013.

Ch. 5

10   O'Conner, Claire. "Undercover Billionaire: Sara Blakely Joins The Rich List Thanks To Spanx." Forbes. https://www.forbes.com/sites/claireoconnor/2012/03/07/undercover-billionaire-sara-blakely-joins-the-rich-list-thanks-to-spanx/#18cd21a6d736 (October 20, 2019).

11   Alba, Jessica. "Our Story." The Honest Company, Inc. https://www.honest.com/about-us/our-story.html (October 20, 2019).

12   Bernstein, Gabrielle. "Meet Gabby." Gabby Bernstein. https://gabbybernstein.com/meet-gabby/ (October 20, 2019).

13   Hipsky, Shellie, "Your Passion, Your Purpose, Your Legacy: An Interview with Dr. Erin." Inspiring Lives Magazine. https://www.inspiringlivesmagazine.com/business/your-

passion-your-purpose-your-legacy-an-interview-with-dr-erin/
(October 20, 2019).

Ch. 6

14   J.K. Rowling. "The Fringe Benefits of Failure, and the
Importance of Imagination." The Harvard Gazette. https://
news.harvard.edu/gazette/story/2008/06/text-of-j-k-rowling-
speech/ (October 20, 2019).

15   Morgan James Publishing. Giving Back. https://www.
morgan-james-publishing.com/giving-back/ (October 20, 2019).

16   Robbins Research International. "About Tony Robbins." Tony Robbins. https://www.tonyrobbins.com/biography/
(October 19, 2019).

Ch. 7

17   Google. Our Approach to Search. https://www.google.
com/search/howsearchworks/mission/ (October 20, 2019).

18   Google. Philosophy. https://www.google.com/about/
philosophy.html (October 20, 2019).

19   Moules, Johnathan. *The Rebel Entrepreneur: Rewriting
the Business Rulebook*. Philadelphia, PA: Kogan Page (2012).

20   Brunson, Russell, *Dot.com Secrets*. New York, NY:
Morgan James Publishing, 2015.

Ch. 8

21   Clifton, Donald O. & Paula Nelson. *Soar with Your
Strengths. New York, NY:* Random House, Inc., 2009.

22   Bolman, Lee G. & Terrence E. Deal. *Leading with
Soul.* San Francisco, CA: Jossey-Bass, 2011.

NOTES

CPSIA information can be obtained
at www.ICGtesting.com
Printed in the USA
JSHW022307250620
6361JS00003B/125

9 781642 798401